Extreme
Government
Makeover

Increasing Our Capacity
to Do More Good

Ken Miller

GOVERNING MANAGEMENT SERIES
Governing Books, Washington, DC

Published by Governing Books
A division of Governing Magazine
1100 Connecticut Ave. NW, Suite 1300
Washington, DC 20036

www.governing.com

The paper used in this publication exceeds the requirements of the American National
Standard for Information Sciences—Permanence of Paper for Printed
Library Materials, ANSI Z39.48-1992.

Printed and bound in the United States of America.

ISBN: 978-0-9833733-0-8

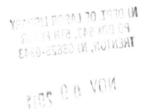

Contents

For Howard. Thanks for inspiring me to write this.
I hope you find it worthy of your recommendation.

FOREWORD

"Life is a journey to see how big our hearts can get."
— Jason Shulman

I'm writing this foreword while watching my incredible wife walk my two beautiful children along the ocean as the sun sets in Waikalua, Hawaii. I am completely overcome with gratitude. Grateful for the little county in Hawaii that brought me here to listen to my musings on government and how it can be great. But I am equally as grateful for my friends in Minneapolis who only want my advice in January. I am grateful for all the public servants around the world who have brought me into their auditoriums, conference rooms, cubicles, and even their homes to learn from me.

But what I am most grateful for is what I have learned from them. The themes in this book — that the work of government is noble, that the people in government are amazing and that we need to turn their passion and creativity toward fixing the broken systems of government — did not come naturally to me. As a management consultant, I first came to government with a very different view. Armed with my MBA and a bag full of private-sector books glorifying warrior CEOs, I was ready to do battle. I unleashed a fury of tactics — performance measures, strategic plans, dashboards, pay-for-performance. Despite my lack of a black belt, I unleashed some amateur Japanese martial arts, hurling Kaizens, hoshin kanris and Ishikawa diagrams left and right. The people of government were the dragon, and I was there to slay them. I would motivate them, hold them accountable and reengineer them to heights they had never scaled before. I was a real piece of work.

Somewhere in my 15-year hero's journey, it all changed for me. It might have been the days I spent working the phones at a child-abuse hotline or the weeks I spent reading case files of chronic abusers. It may have been walking the wards at the Sexual Offender Treatment Center or doing the focus groups with staff at the Home for the Criminally Insane. Heck, it was probably the one day a month I worked the counter at the DMV. Whatever it was, it changed me. It thawed my heart and then broke it wide open.

They say the goal of religion is to help you walk this earth with a soft heart. Or, as the modern mystic Jason Shulman puts it, "Life is a journey to see how big our hearts can get." Well, I got religion. And it turned out that the public servants I thought I was saving ended up saving me.

This book is that religion — my beliefs and worldview on increasing the public sector's capacity to do good — and I want to share that religion with all the zealotry of a recent convert.

I didn't invent these beliefs. They're not new. In fact, they have existed for centuries, in cultures all across the globe. The concepts have been contemplated, taught, and protected by mystics on every continent. They are the systems thinkers — Ackoff, Goldratt, Deming, Scholtes, Block, Senge, Lawton, Seddon. What they teach is a radical departure from the command-and-control structures that permeate modern organizational life. Instead, the focus is on the invisible structure, the systems that exist to get the work done. Our results come from our systems. Our systems are shaped by our beliefs. It's only when we make these systems visible, and make our beliefs visible, that we can change them. This way of thinking has healing powers — for the organization, its customers, and its employees. And we need it now more than ever.

So why has government been so resistant to change? So hard to improve? Because to truly change something, you have to love it. Empathy, compassion, and love are what transform. Disdain, judgment, and disrespect won't change anything. Most people who have tried to improve government have done it from a lofty perch, outside the walls, lobbing grenades at it. They talk about everything that's wrong with public servants. They expose millions in waste, and they prescribe tried-and-true private-sector solutions. They get nowhere. They expose and ridicule and wonder why no healing takes place. Would you swallow a pill from someone who just slapped you? Our transformation will come from the inside, from the dedicated public servants who love their work. Change will come from those who don't see it as work, but as a cause, a ministry, a way to make a difference.

The real power in life is not what's in your head but what is in your heart. Nothing in this book will help you until you change your heart. Some of you are already there, and some may convert after reading. Wherever you are, I invite you, before you begin this book, to change the lens. To see government with fresh eyes. To acknowledge that:

The work of government is noble.
The people of government are amazing.
The systems of government are a mess.

Let's work together to make them great.

— Ken Miller

CHAPTER 1
This Old House

In the summer of 2007, I made a decision that would alter my worldview forever. I had spent the better part of ten years traveling across the country, working with government agencies to help them find ways to do their vital work 80 percent faster. Living in Jefferson City, Missouri, the nearest airport was two hours away in St. Louis. I spent most of those frequent two-hour drives dodging orange cones and 18-wheel semis, as I-70 was one of the most traveled and treacherous roadways in the United States.

One evening, after semi-consciously arriving in my garage following a two-hour bout of highway hypnosis, I told my wife it was time to move. If traveling and speaking were going to be my life, I needed to move closer to an airport so the drive wouldn't cost me my life. Amazingly, she agreed. And with that, I ripped out the fourteen years of roots my wife had planted in Jefferson City and relocated the family to Kansas City, ten minutes from the most passenger-friendly airport in the world.

The relocation prompted a spiritual journey into what really matters in life, but this book isn't about that. Nor is it about the pain and sacrifice endured by an amazing woman in order to support me. (Maybe those books will come later.)

No, this book is about the fourteen months of hell we endured building a house — and what that experience ultimately taught me about life, government, people, time, and the capacity to do great things.

In retrospect, our first mistake was the decision to build a house rather than buying from existing stock. (It was 2007, and houses were still expensive. Had we waited a year, we could have bought two houses.) Our stated reason for building was that we wanted to delight in creating a home that we ourselves had designed, a home that completely met our needs and matched our tastes. I later learned the real reason we built was that my wife (bless her) wasn't yet ready to let go of her community, and she'd hoped that the building process would delay the move for a while. She definitely got her wish.

One of the first builders we met was a decent gentleman. (The fact that I'm using those two words ought to foreshadow that we ultimately went with someone else.) He had a good eye for design, and, even better, he'd been on the show *Extreme Makeover: Home Edition*. In fact, he'd been on three times.

For those of you who have never seen the show, it's quite an amazing thing to watch. In the early episodes of the series, the crew of professional designers and builders would surprise a deserving family with some home repairs. I remember one Season 1 episode that centered on a man whose sister had passed away, leaving her six children without a family. He had decided to adopt all six kids and raise them in his home. Unfortunately, he lived in a house with just one bedroom. *Extreme Makeover* to the rescue! The team swooped in and transformed his home, making it the kind of place a man with that big of a heart could raise that big of a family.

That was Season 1. As the series has progressed, the crew now doesn't just modify homes. Instead, they show up, knock the old house down, and build a brand-new, beautiful home in the same spot — in seven days!

Surely a man capable of doing that three times could get my family to Kansas City before school started in the fall. So it was with great enthusiasm that I asked him, "Kevin, when will our house be finished?" I figured seven days, plus a few weather delays, plus a little slack time here and there. Three months, tops.

His answer? "Nine months."

Nine months? What happened to seven days? "Oh, we don't do them all that way," he said.

My wife and I met with several more builders, eventually settling on a man we came to call El Diablo. Fourteen months, 200 broken promises, three mediated settlements, and an endless string of apartments and hotel rooms later, our family began its new life. Ah, the American Dream.

So what's all this got to do with government? Nothing, I just needed to vent. No, in all seriousness, my tale of construction woes actually has everything to do with government. As I watched my home not being built, I saw subcontractors disappearing and my savings account steadily depleting (along with my wife's legendary patience). I kept thinking that there simply had to be a better way — a better way to manage, communicate, and get things done. And now, as I watch the work of government, I see good-hearted people dispirited, bold agendas dashed, lines of people waiting, out-of-control costs, and endless complexity. I keep thinking that there has to be a better way — a better way to manage, communicate, and get things done.

As this book unfolds, you will see that there is indeed a better way. A better way to get the vital work of government done. A better way to engage the hearts and minds of public servants. To deal with the crushing demand on government services, to meet these demands with fewer resources, and to ensure that the operations of government live up to the noble ideals of government.

There is a way to do all this. To do the work of government 80 percent faster, better, and at a lower cost. And the secrets are all contained in that one reality TV show. The house of government needs a makeover, and an extreme one. And just as on that show, we need it fast. Because from everything I'm seeing, we are out of ideas.

Exhibit A: The Contest

The Obama administration, like every other new administration, came into office with a bold agenda and lofty, often contentious goals. As a staff full of policy wonks and idealists migrated from the campaign trail to the executive branch, they were quickly greeted with a bucket of red ink. Like nearly every other government at the end of the first decade of this century, the federal government was broke. Some big decisions needed to be made about where to cut costs and find savings.

The White House's answer? A contest. Yep, a contest for all federal employees to come up with the best idea to save money. I'm not picking on Obama or taking political shots here. This misguided initiative has been promulgated by administrations of every party at every level of government. The reason I'm highlighting this contest in particular is because of the entry that ultimately won, and what that says about the current state of thinking. The winning idea was chosen by a panel of judges from over 30,000 submissions nationwide. And what was the idea? Get your pencils ready, because here it is: Patients being discharged from veterans hospitals should be allowed to take home any unused portions of their prescriptions.

I'll give you a moment to finish jotting that one down.

I received a hundred emails the day that idea won. People were shaking their collective heads, laughing, and they wanted me to pile on. But I couldn't. I found the whole thing too sad to be funny. Was it a good, common-sense idea? Yep. Will it save our debt-riddled republic? Not even close. And remember, this was the best idea.

Exhibit B: Private-Sector Panaceas

There seems to be a prevailing wisdom that good ideas only come from the private sector, and that we in government could solve all our problems if only we would listen to them. It's as if the private sector is a race of aliens who hold the secrets to life and are in possession of ideas and technologies that could greatly benefit our primitive government culture. Occasionally, one of these aliens crash-lands into the public-sector bureaucracy and shares the secrets of his race.

In 2010, one gubernatorial candidate campaigned through her state with a prop: paper clips. She would hold up paper clips at her speeches and remind the voters how much money was spent by wasteful bureaucrats on paper clips. She actually made one large state department count its paper clips. All of them. All 423,000. Plus 37,601 binder clips and 17,425 pens. (The cost of tallying those figures surely rivaled the actual cost of the items themselves.) But it gets better. The solution the candidate devised was to create an online, Craigslist-style office-supply exchange, in which your need for legal pads could be matched with someone who is hoarding legal pads.

Mind you, the economy and budget of this particular state had been eviscerated by a collapse in the housing market, a gutting of property taxes, and one of the worst declines in tourism in generations. Saving on office supplies wasn't going to do the trick.

It's not just that this idea is colossally stupid and insulting. It's what it says about the private and public sectors. You see, when I first heard this story, I experienced a vivid flashback to my time in state government. One of my first suicide missions in government improvement was trying to get regulatory agencies in my department to adopt a Total Quality Management approach. I found a great friend and sympathizer at the agency that regulated banks. He, like me, had been "volunteered" for the TQM steering committee, and within twenty-four months he had squandered twenty years of goodwill with upper management and was forced to move on to an executive job at a bank. We were having lunch one day, and he told me of the visit he'd had the previous day with his bank's CEO. (This was not a small regional bank, by the way. This was a national conglomerate, and the CEO was in town on a countrywide cost-cutting road show.) The CEO's solution? Paper clips. Apparently, he had a well-rehearsed whiteboard exercise in which he'd ask how many people worked in the local office, and then, using highly advanced calculus, he'd tabulate the annual cost of paper clips, pens and Post-It notes the employees were wasting. His credo: Pens, chain 'em down; paper clips, leave 'em in the drawer; Post-Its, bring 'em from home. (In 2009, U.S. taxpayers bailed this bank out for nearly a billion dollars. I guess they were using way too many paper clips.)

The gubernatorial candidate was, of course, an ex-banker. The fact that she was focused on paper clips is extremely telling. (Again, this is non-partisan; both parties do it.) The reason elected officials and private-sector executives rarely have good ideas for improving government isn't because they're dumb. It's because they're blind.

The real costs and opportunities in government are hidden. The operations of government are complex, difficult to understand, and usually invisible. (I'll talk more about this idea in Chapter 3.) As I argued in my previous book, *We Don't Make Widgets*, it's often hard to see what government does. In manufacturing, you can easily see the factory, the widget it's producing, the customers, and the bottom line. But in government, those concepts are extraordinarily complicated (unless, of course, you read my book). Government is made up of hard-working people trapped in dysfunctional systems, producing invisible things for people who often don't want them, for reasons we rarely articulate and can hardly measure.

The net result is that the work of government is intangible and hard to see. Consequently, people trying to cut costs tend to focus on the things that are tangible and easy to see, things such as buildings, fleet cars, cell phones, organizational charts, and, of course, paper clips. But these items didn't cause the crisis in government, and they won't yield the solution.

Exhibit C: The Consolidation Crutch

In 2010, one of the nation's larger cities was facing an extraordinary budget deficit, a $1.5 billion gap on a $63 billion budget. The city hired a new deputy mayor who set out to find efficiencies. Looking under all the usual rocks — office space, office supplies, fleet vehicles, and org charts — he surfaced with a report promising to save $500 million, or $125 million per year for four years. Remarkable: a 0.01 percent savings. And all the city had to do to achieve the 0.01 percent savings was to wrest control over facilities, fleet, personnel, and technology from eighteen independent, politically connected, powerful departments. Piece of cake.

Nearly every effort to find efficiencies arrives at the same solution: consolidation. Wherever there are two or more doing the same function, there should be one. It seems to make common sense. Shouldn't we have just one HR unit? One IT shop? One print center and one vehicle maintenance garage? But there are two major problems with this approach.

First, the pain required to consolidate far exceeds any cost savings. Imagine for a second that you're the mayor of a large city. Under you are ten departments with ten strong-willed managers. You have a bold agenda to dramatically impact the lives of the people in your community, and you need a unified team to pull it off. Now I come to you with the following proposal: I can save you 0.01 percent of your total budget by consolidating similar functions. In return, all you have to do is devote the rest of your term to fighting with the very people you need to help you implement your agenda. You will have to use all your political capital to pry their hands off their HR,

The Consolidating Game

Still think consolidation is the answer? Let me fast-forward five years for you. The really powerful divisions (coincidentally, the ones where you had anticipated the biggest cost savings) will get around the consolidation. Inside all the other newly consolidated departments, little in-house HR, IT, and fleet shops will begin to emerge. It starts small, but eventually the departments will recreate what has been taken from them. And you end up worse than when you started: Each department still has its own functions, and now you have a centralized bureaucracy as well.

IT, and support resources. You will spend all your time in senior staff meetings defending your decisions. In addition, all your one-on-one time with the department heads will be spent granting exceptions to the consolidation plan. When we're finished, five years later, we will have consolidated the departments (except for the stubborn ones who managed to exempt themselves), saved a little less than 0.01 percent, and destroyed any goodwill you had as a leader. Up for it?

If the reward were substantial enough, you might be. But overhead in government — all the offices, supplies, fleets, HR functions, and so on — adds up to roughly 10 percent of the total budget. The most ambitious consolidation efforts are going to yield a 1 percent savings, at best. And they come at the cost of dissension, division, and a wasted agenda.

The other problem with the consolidation-is-king argument is that consolidation ultimately hurts productivity. Our most precious resource in government is our capacity to do good. Consolidation reduces this capacity.

Think about it: Suppose I told you that your life could be vastly more efficient if you ditched your car, got rid of your cell phone and sold your house. After all, you only use your car a couple times a day. You're only on your cell phone a few hours a day (unless you happen to be a teenage girl). And think about how many square feet of your house go unused most of the time — what a waste! To become efficient, you should consolidate those activities with other people. Use a public payphone whenever you need to make a call. Share a car with ten of your friends. Move out of your private home and into a communal living facility, where everyone shares the kitchen and bathrooms.

If you did all those things you could save some money. So why don't you? Because you'd have a hell of a time getting anything done. Sometimes we sacrifice efficiency for productivity. But that's only half the story.

Now imagine not only that you have to use payphones, a carpool, and a commune, but that they're all run by monopolies that don't care about your needs. Lots of people waiting to use that payphone? Better get in line, because the phone company's not adding another one. Expecting a new baby in your family? Well, that commune's only got so much room, so you'll have to make do. Consolidations create monopolies. We hate monopolies. Monopolies treat customers like hostages. This is the real reason agencies resist consolidation. They know they'll have to deal with a monopoly in order to get anything done. Imagine if your professional success depended on the cable company, the postal service, US Airways, and the local school board. Good luck.

On top of that, consolidation efforts usually mean a double-whammy for agencies. Individual agencies will be held accountable for results, but they suddenly have no control over the technology, equipment, personnel, or finances it takes to achieve those results. Powerless accountability is a recipe for disaster.

Getting to Work

Again, it's not so much that any of these ideas are bad. It's just that they are hopelessly trivial. The house of government doesn't need new paint on the shutters or a new doorbell. Our problems are way bigger than that. Upon inspection, our house has two serious problems.

First, our pipes. The pipes of government — our systems, operations, and processes — are a mess. They're kinked up, rusted out, and about to burst. Ravaged by years of budget cuts, reorganizations, and half-finished technology projects, the systems of government simply don't have the capacity to keep up. We can't get the water to those who need it. Consequently, the pipes are leaking, water-pressure is building, and there's an ever-growing group of people on our front porch waiting for us to help them.

Second, we've got mold. Everywhere. Moldy thinking. Old ideas about people and motivation. We've come to believe that the problems with government are "people problems" — that public servants are lazy, unmotivated, and need to be incentivized to do the right thing. Oh, we don't say it that way. Instead, we call it "pay for performance" or we create competency models and performance development plans. But the message to employees is the same: Government will improve when you improve. This moldy view of people has given rise to the accountability movement. And just like real mold, this movement has spoiled the air, damaged the foundation, and is making everyone sick.

The two problems in our house are obviously related. The moldy thinking kinks our pipes, and slow, backed-up pipes create more calls for accountability, and so on and so on. This book addresses both problems head-on. If we are ever going to do all the good in the world that government can do, we have to increase our capacity. And our capacity comes from our pipes. This book will show you in great detail how to find your pipes and radically redesign them. But fixing the pipes without eradicating the mold will do us no good. Before we can transform our operations, we have to transform our beliefs about people, about government, and about what is possible.

What This Book Is Not

This is not a bash-the-government book written by someone who doesn't understand government or, worse, doesn't like it. I don't believe, as one of our presidents said, that government is the problem. Nor do I believe we are the solution. But we are *part* of the solution. We are educating children, protecting the environment, protecting the peace, and giving help to people who need it. We are protecting the most vulnerable, preserving the outdoors, and building the infrastructure that keeps the world's greatest economy moving. The work of government is noble.

This is also not a book where we bash the people of government. There are no calls for outsourcing or privatization or childish employee-engagement programs like Throwing Fish or Employee of the Month. What I've seen in my two decades working with the public sector is that the people of government are amazing. They work long hours at child-abuse hotlines listening to the most unimaginable calls. They work dangerous shifts in maximum-security prisons and psychiatric wards. They broker adoptions, protect public health, and counsel struggling businesses. Sure, there are high-profile bad apples: the idiot who takes the city-owned car to the strip bar, the manager who uses her state-issued credit card like it's her personal bank account. But those people are, by far, the exception to the rule. The vast majority of public servants are hard workers who toil for that noblest of causes: making a difference in people's lives.

This also isn't a political book. Democrat, Republican, liberal, conservative: There are well-meaning people with great ideas on both sides of the aisle. There are also flame-throwing crazies with bad intentions whose only desire is to move the political football one yard into enemy territory. The political system is not going to change, no matter how many tea parties we throw or how loudly we chant "yes we can!" And honestly, I'm not concerned. The real opportunity to improve government isn't at the political level with the policymakers. Rather, it's in the pipes — the performance of government — with the plant managers. While the policymakers fight about whether food stamps are good or bad, the plant managers are figuring out how to serve 40 percent more families 80 percent faster with fewer resources. While politicians debate about whether industry is over- or under-regulated, the plant managers are figuring out how to balance the competing interests of multiple stakeholders and deliver environmental permits faster and with better clarity. While elected officials demagogue tax cuts or increases, plant managers are figuring out how to collect all the money that is owed, simplify tax filing, and refund taxpayers their hard-earned money 80 percent faster.

There is no doubt that politics and policy impact operations. But we also know that we can't do anything about that. This book is not filled with academic speculation about how to end partisan rancor or get politicians to care about performance. (They rarely do.) Nor do I prescribe some budgeting method that presupposes elected officials will make vital resource allocation decisions based on logic and rational thought. (They rarely do.) No, I'm not going to argue with reality, and the reality is that the political level rarely cares about performance. (That is, until something goes wrong. Then, rather than using it as a chance to improve the pipes, politicians instead use the incident as a lead pipe with which to bludgeon the other side.) This doesn't mean they shouldn't care; they definitely should. Politicians take office with grand intentions. They want to tackle new stuff, big stuff. However, our ability to tackle big new issues is influenced by how well we are handling the old issues. For example, the 2010 health-care debate was framed by cogent arguments along the lines of, "You want the people who run the post office and the DMV to run your hospital?" Our government friends in Canada have a great motto: "Performance Equals Trust." People's trust in government to solve problems (currently at an all-time low) is shaped by their experience with the performance of government. If we can't get citizens a birth certificate before they get their death certificate, they will rightly question our ability to improve health access.

Politicians also need to care about performance for one other simple reason — capacity. Newly elected officials quickly realize they can't accomplish any of their big plans because the pipes of government have no more capacity. Politicians want programs to improve family self-sufficiency, but the social workers are maxed out. They want to increase literacy, but the teachers are maxed out. I sympathize with all the elected officials right now who will basically spend their entire terms in office figuring out how to shrink the pipes, not how to quench thirst. If they're ever going to get to their agendas, someone has to figure out how to move a ton of water through some very narrow, kinked-up pipes. And that is exactly what this book is about. The systems of government are a mess. We can stand around arguing about whether the house of government is too big or costs too much, whether it's a fixer-upper or a money pit. Or we can grab some tools and join the crew. Love it or hate it, we can't sell it, and we're not moving. Instead, let's work together to give this deserving home a much-needed makeover.

CHAPTER 2

A Pipe Dream

The problems that currently plague government performance seem almost insurmountable:

- rising costs
- slashed budgets
- failed IT projects
- critical mistakes
- low morale
- low customer satisfaction
- labor-management strife
- long lines
- huge backlogs.

(Not to mention the supercharged political environment, the collapse of traditional media, and the aging workforce that's about to walk out the door with every bit of institutional knowledge crammed in their brown hard-shell briefcases.)

So how can we even begin to solve all these problems? By recognizing that they are all symptoms of one problem: capacity. Simply, government does not have the capacity to do everything it needs to do, or everything its citizens want it to do. The demands on government far exceed its capacity, which in turn leads to budget shortfalls, long lines, low morale and, as I will discuss shortly, all the other problems I listed above.

Perhaps a simple analogy will help. Think of the work of government as a set of water pipes. For example, a pipe that distributes food stamps or environmental permits; one that spits out court orders or filled potholes; one for adoption placements, one for defense contracts and so on. For every service, a pipe. At one end is the faucet. That's the demand. The faucet is turned on and the water flows through the pipe, eventually coming out the other end for the recipient to drink. The work of government is the pipes.

What is happening today is simple to understand: The pipes of government have stayed the same size or become narrower, while the faucet has been cranked wide open. In human services alone (things like food stamps, unemployment, and child care), the demand has increased by over 40 percent in the past three years, while the size of the pipes (in this case, the workforce handling the services) has decreased by 20 percent. The result? A flood of water stuck in the pipes, constantly backing up, building pressure, and leaking out of the holes.

This is happening everywhere in government right now, at every agency, every level, every jurisdiction. Government really only has one problem — a capacity problem. If we had the capacity to keep up with demand, then customers wouldn't be yelling at us, employees wouldn't be stressed out, things wouldn't fall through the cracks, new initiatives could be implemented, and bold agendas could be embraced. But we don't. And we won't. This is the new normal for the public sector.

When you realize government's capacity problem, you also quickly see only two possible solutions. You can either reduce the amount of water coming in or increase the size of the pipes. Unfortunately for government, neither of those is going to happen. Despite decades of alternating liberal or conservative leadership, the size and scope of government — what we're trying to accomplish, who we're trying to help — continue to grow. What is not growing, however, and probably won't for another generation, is the size of the pipes. At best, agencies have been able to maintain a stable workforce size. At worst, they are seeing annual workforce reductions of 10 to 20 percent. At the same time citizens are calling on the government to do more for them, they're faced with fewer people to help. So we can't make the pipes any bigger, and we can't turn off the faucet. Seems hopeless.

Except, there is a third option — one that reveals itself only when you rip out the walls, tear up the floors, and expose the pipes themselves. See, ideally, our pipes would be relatively straight and simple. Say a citizen needs a birth certificate. She fills out an order; it flows through a short, straight pipe; and she gets her certificate in no time. Or think about a state contractor who needs to get paid. He submits an invoice; it flows through a short, straight pipe; and he gets his check in very little time.

In reality, though, our pipes don't look anything like this. Rather than being short and straight, they are long and twisted. The water that comes out of the faucet is plunged down a waterslide of twists, drop-offs, sudden stops, and loop-de-loops. And instead of thirty seconds of harrowing excitement, we drag that wild ride into thirty days, six months, or sometimes even years. And the faucet just keeps pumping more and more water into the system.

The systems of government — the pipes — are a mess. They're kinked up by decades of specialization, reorganizations, cover-your-ass (CYA) efforts, cost-cutting, and abandoned technology projects. They've been outsourced, in-sourced, downsized, right-sized, and zero-based budgeted. And now they're so twisted and slow, they make a silly straw look efficient.

Because the pipes are so twisted, kinked, and gummed-up, there's very little water that can move through them. There's a firehose at one end but only a trickle coming out the other.

We all saw evidence of this in the summer of 2009, with the federal stimulus program. Our economy was apparently on the brink of collapse. And, without getting into a Keynes/Friedman debate, the

The Tax Refund Roller Coaster

Every year around the middle of May, people start wondering where their tax refunds are. The government has had their money long enough; it's time to buy a new TV. How hard can it be to give you your money back? It really isn't that hard. The tasks themselves are quite simple:

- Open the return
- Sort the contents
- Do a quick quality check
- Enter the return into a computer system
- Print and send a check.

For most tax agencies I have worked with, that adds up to about three to five minutes of actual work. So why can't you get your refund five minutes after you mail it in? Because the pipes are an absolute mess.

Picture yourself as your tax return. First, you're sent to a large mail-processing center, where you wait in a postal tub until your turn. Then you're scooped up with a pile of other returns and run through a large centralized mail-opening machine. You get grouped with at least ninety-nine other tax-return forms (and you should get to know each other, since you'll be traveling the entire length of this pipe government's solution was to spend lots of money very quickly in order to jolt the economy back into action. Anyone who works in government could have forecast what would happen. Government may spend a lot, but quickly? Sure enough, six months into the stimulus, there was a great hue and cry about where the money had gone. Why were there no roads being constructed? Why were there no new

together). Your group is loaded onto a truck and delivered to another facility, where another specialist will prepare you to be entered into the system. Your group will be assigned a cover sheet, and you will get stamped with a number in case you get lost. You and your group will wait for some time before being entered into the system — either by being keyed in or by having your image taken. But get ready to wait, since there aren't enough imaging machines or key-entry staff. Once your picture has been taken, your paper self will sit around in a file until someone gets around to archiving you. Your digital self waits in a queue until the large mainframe computer is ready to process you. If you had been a tax return that was paying the government, you would be processed immediately. But since you want a refund, you will be processed on the weekend or later.

Before your check can be printed, another agency has to intervene to ensure there is enough money in the Treasury to pay you. Once that agency has given its blessing, a check is printed at *another* agency, stuffed in an envelope and brought to your door by the U.S. Postal Service.

Total time? Two weeks, maybe two months, maybe even longer. But the actual labor time stayed the same: about five minutes.

bridges opening or small businesses starting? They were all stuck in the pipes.

The stimulus program was another crank on the faucet. Unfortunately, all that new water just got stuck in the pipes, behind the older water that hadn't yet completed its journey. New roads? That's at least a five-year pipe. New bridges? Same thing. Create small business loans, find the entrepreneurs, certify their plans, complete credit work, and support the start-up? Two years at least. The pipes of government were at full capacity when the stimulus began. How could the new water possibly make it through any faster?

The Invisible Solution

Capacity is the problem, and pipes are the culprit. So what's the solution? How do we get more water to move through the pipes?

The answer is simple: Straighten the pipes.

Think about it. When you're trying to water your plants and the water isn't moving through the hose quickly enough, what do you do? You straighten the hose. When the gas isn't getting in your tank fast enough, what do you do? You straighten the pump. When the Army Corps of Engineers wants to speed up a river, what do they do? They straighten it.

When you bend a pipe, a hose, or a river, you slow down the flow. Slower flow means less gets through. But when you straighten a pipe, a hose, or a river, you speed the flow. Faster flow means more gets through. How can we do more in government? Straighten the pipes. Speed the flow. The faster the water moves through the pipes, the more that gets done at less cost.

It's such a simple concept. Straighten the pipes. Take out the kinks, the twists and turns and endless loops. Recover the simplicity that used to exist. Get the water to flow the shortest, straightest route. Simple. So why don't we do this in government? Why don't we straighten the pipes? Because we don't see them.

I remember one of the first homes my wife and I lived in. A classic fixer-upper, this house had been "reorganized" many times. I kept walking on the carpet in the living room and getting my sock wet in a certain spot. The first four times, I blamed the dog. The fifth time, I actually looked up. And there, coming out of the drywall ceiling, was a tiny drop of water. I immediately called a roofer and prepared to kiss my dream of a newer car goodbye. But the roofer couldn't find anything wrong and suggested I call a plumber. "A plumber?" I said. "What for? We don't have a toilet or shower anywhere near this room, especially not above it."

Well, I called a plumber anyway. Sure enough, he discovered that during one of the many reorganizations, a pipe had been routed over the top of the living room, a joint was faulty, and the water was slowly dripping through the ceiling. I never would have guessed there would be a pipe there. (We also hoped the next owners wouldn't guess there was a pipe there either. Because rather than repairing the ceiling, we placed a fake air-vent over the hole and conveniently forgot to mention it.)

Unless you are trained to look, the pipes of government are invisible. Just as in my living room, we only see the pipes when they burst. We only really see the systems of government when something goes terribly wrong. And then, rather than fixing the pipes, we engage in a collective blame storm.

We all experienced this very phenomenon just after Christmas of 2009, when the now-infamous "underwear bomber" tried to blow up a flight bound for Detroit. I don't mean to make light of a serious issue, but the entire episode offers a lesson in "seeing the pipes." The terrorist had hidden some form of incendiary device in his underpants before boarding the plane. On board, he began stripping down in his seat and trying to catch himself on fire.

Understandably, this caught the attention of another passenger, who promptly pummeled the terrorist and saved Christmas for all. Many of you, basking in the glow of new gadgets and eggnog-fueled holiday parties, may have missed what happened next. The secretary of Homeland Security held a press conference in which she confidently proclaimed that "the system worked." The news media were astonished, as was I. If by "the system," she meant "vigilant passengers with a keen eye for exploding undergarments risking their life at the last second," then we're all in serious trouble. Wisely, President Obama stepped in and made it clear that "the system did not work." He then went on to explain why. After hearing his detailed description of all the different computer databases, cross-matches, watch lists, update times, transfer logs, international policies, and even time-zone differences, I was amazed we could *ever* stop a terrorist from boarding a plane. The No-Fly List pipe was an absolute mess.

As the president talked, I kept envisioning the twisted pipe. The media did not. All they asked — twenty-four hours a day for three straight days, on every cable news channel — was whom the president would fire. Who will be responsible for this? Someone had to be blamed.

As a systems thinker, I was overjoyed by the president's response. Whom would he fire? Whom *could* he fire? The entire system was broken. The pipe was a mess from beginning to end. The pipe cut across bureaus, departments, and countries. Whom could you fire? Fixing the system would take time and effort. That was no fun for the media. They like to have a crime, a culprit, and an execution wrapped up in a week. The president saw systems. The media saw people.

So why do we always blame the people? Because we can see them. They are tangible. Systems are invisible. It's hard to improve what you can't see. So we focus our attention on the things that are visible.

How We See Government

We tend to see government in two ways: physically and fiscally. Physically, government is a collection of buildings, fleet vehicles, radios, cell phones, copiers, paper, and office supplies. Fiscally, government is a collection of departments, programs, bureaus, sections, funds, budget categories, and cost sections. When you try to improve only what you can *physically* see, the solutions are fairly limited: Count it, automate it, consolidate it, upgrade it, modernize it, buy less of it, or get rid of it. The solutions are similarly limited when you focus just on what you can *fiscally* see: Reorganize it, measure it, plan it, budget it, and hold it accountable.

Neither view helps solve our capacity problem. In fact, those "solutions" compound the problem. Their prescriptions for efficiency actually kink the pipes and slow us down. Our reorganized, consolidated, centralized, balanced-scorecard-managed, outcome-based-budgeted agencies now take a whole lot longer to do a whole lot more work just a tiny bit more cheaply.

With both the physical and fiscal viewpoints, what you see most is people. Physically, you see them coming into work, paving a street, or standing on the corner smoking. Fiscal types see FTEs, filled positions, and vacancies. Because the people are what's visible, they get most of the attention when it comes to improving government. We try to motivate them, incentivize them, train them, and change them. We want them to do more, and do it faster. We want them productive, smiling, and adaptable. As I'll explain in Chapter 3, these attempts don't work. But even if they did, they're built on a false premise — the idea that improving individual performance improves organizational performance. That if everyone would just peddle harder and faster, the organization would get where it needs to go. As W. Edwards Deming, the grandfather of the quality movement, proved years ago, "Six percent of the problems we experience can be traced back to people. Ninety-four percent are inside the system." The variation, constraints, and problems are in the pipes.

In *The Leader's Handbook,* my favorite management thinker, Peter Scholtes, puts it more bluntly, with my all-time favorite quote:

> All of the empowered, motivated, teamed-up, self-directed, incentivized, accountable, reengineered and reinvented people you can muster cannot compensate for a dysfunctional system. When the system is functioning well, these other things are all just foofaraw. When the system is not functioning well, these things are still only empty, meaningless twaddle.

Need proof that a personnel-focused approach won't work? Just look around. We've been using these strategies forever. We give them new names and try a lot harder, but the end result is the same: a lot of effort expended for a minimal impact. Costs are still out of control, customers are still waiting, and the ability to do new things is thwarted. Every crisis, we turn over the same rocks. To get through our capacity crisis, we need to look under a different rock.

What Do We Mean By 'Systems,' Anyway?

Inside all the departments, programs, bureaus, and sections are systems, the methods we use to accomplish results. Systems are the processes, policies, procedures, and skills we use to get work done. They are the pipes. They're invisible from 30,000 feet, but from underground you can see them connecting the departments and programs, the technology and people. Systems are what we are really funding, and systems are what consume all our resources. Systems are where the employees work and the customers show up. The systems are where we create value, and the systems are where our capacity to do that is most constrained.

So what exactly is a system?

Every system is composed of these four elements:

Purpose: the results or desired outcomes of the system. Why it exists. *Why we do it.*

Deliverable: the "thing" that is produced by the system. It is that which will pop out at the end of the process, that which is delivered to the customer/user. (It's what I refer to as the "widget" in *We Don't Make Widgets.*) The deliverable is *what we do.*

Customer/user: the person or people who will use the deliverable of the system. It's by their using the deliverable that the system achieves its purpose. They are *who we do it for or who we do it to.*

Process: how the deliverable is produced. It includes the policies, procedures, methods, tools, technologies, and, of course, people. This is where the work occurs. It's *how we do it.*

Of course, we could go back even further to look at the suppliers of the systems and the inputs they provide as well. But the four elements above form the essence of any system: what we do, how we do it, who we do it for, and why.

Systems and their four components are easiest to understand in terms of manufacturing. It's all very tangible in the widget world. If you've ever visited a factory, you've seen the system from the front door to the back door. A truck shows up at one door and drops off supplies and materials. Workers toil away in the processes, manufacturing a perfect widget that then gets loaded on another truck to be delivered to a happy customer. And the purpose of that system is quite simple as well: to make money. Factory, widget, customer, profit. Process, deliverable, user, results. Pipes, water, drinker, quenched thirst. Pick the image that works best for you. What matters is that we begin to see the work as a system.

All work, in fact, is a system. Whether you're a plant manager producing cars, a priest delivering sermons, a doctor prescribing a treatment or a bureau chief cranking out reports, your work is a system. An organization is simply a collection of systems designed to achieve a result. There are big systems and small systems. Systems inside of systems. Systems that feed other systems. For me, and for the purpose of this book, it's easiest to visualize systems as pipes. Instead of org charts and mission statements, I seek to see the pipes of an agency. What is the main pipe? Which pipe is the essence of this agency? Which pipes enable or constrain that pipe? Which pipes consume all the resources? Which pipes cause all the customer problems? Which pipes cause all the phone calls? Behind every organizational problem is a set of pipes gone amok. Once you start seeing life this way, you're able to look past the paper clips, org charts, and people programs and grasp the real opportunity that comes from radically improving systems.

Strategies to Improve Systems

The strategies to improve systems are not industry-specific. They work in health care, government, education, and everywhere else. Essentially, you must:

1. Ensure you are in the right business. This is the field of innovation. Innovation (which is different from continuous improvement) is about focusing on your "purpose" and thinking of new ways to accomplish it. Continuous improvement led Franklin to make better day planners and AAA to make better maps. *Innovation* created the Blackberry and GPS devices. Innovation recognizes that the purpose of food stamps is to help reduce food insecurity and then thinks of other ways to bring people and food together. Innovation recognizes that environmental permits exist to balance the competing priorities of a growing economy and a safe environment and then figures out different ways to meet these challenges.

2. Understand the customers and their needs. Quality is defined by the customer. And what customers generally want are widgets that are easy to use, timely, affordable, and reliable. Customers also want choice. Of course, all of these are moot if the customers can't achieve their desired outcomes. The best way to uncover customer priorities is to actively engage your customers in designing better systems and continuously seek their feedback and ideas.

3. Build a better widget. Results come through our systems. We obtain those results by customers' using our widgets. Whether the widgets are driver licenses, building permits, speeding tickets, WIC vouchers, or mental health assessments, it's only through customers' successfully *using* them that we get safe highways, safe buildings, healthy infants, and improved quality of life. If you aren't happy with your results, build a better widget.

4. Improve the process. Notice that this is last in the sequence. It does little good to make better, faster, and cheaper that which we should not make at all. When we are sure we're in the right business, sure that we're giving customers what they want, sure that the widget is the best it can be, then we can set about the hard work of building the widgets faster, with fewer mistakes and at less cost.

Once you recognize you have a system, then these techniques apply to you. As the "plant manager" for your widget, you should be doing these four things all the time. If, for example, you produce policies, make sure they are good ones. They need to be clear, concise, and comprehensive. Make sure the customers of the policies have input and can easily access and use them. Make sure the policy makes the desired outcome easier to obtain. And by God make it fast. While you are stewing on it, editing, revising it, arguing about it, and figuring out how to CYA, there are people in the field paralyzed with inaction and customers who can't be helped.

If you produce environmental permits, then make sure they're good ones. They need to be clear, concise, and easy to understand. Make sure the customers of the permits have input and can easily access them and use them. Make sure the permits achieve the desired outcome (in this case, a clean environment). And by God make them fast. While you're stewing, editing, reviewing, reviewing, and reviewing, there are businesses waiting to open and jobs waiting to be filled.

Or if, say, you produce street repairs, then make sure they're good ones. They should be unobtrusive and long-lasting. Make sure the customers are inconvenienced as little as possible. Make sure the repairs achieve the desired outcome (a safe, efficient transportation system). And by God make them fast. While you're staring at the hole, going back to the shed for different equipment, and getting called away on four other emergencies, we drivers are piling up behind orange barrels screaming at the people in front of us.

For our purposes, we're going to focus primarily on one of the four components: the process/factory/pipes. It's not because the other three aren't important. It is absolutely essential that we focus on innovation and customer satisfaction, and that the widget we produce is easy to use, accurate, reliable, cost-effective, and of high quality. Those three system components are absolutely vital, but they're not the emphasis of this book for a couple reasons.

First, I covered them in depth in *We Don't Make Widgets*. In that book, you can learn about:

- Turning intangible service work into tangible widgets
- Measuring the seemingly immeasurable
- Determining who the customer is
- Segmenting customers by the role they play
- Why customer satisfaction matters when the customers have no choice
- Why customer service is not enough
- How to measure customer satisfaction without surveys

- Defining your bottom line and measuring results
- A systematic process to get outside the box and develop innovative alternatives to your current offerings.

The other reason this book focuses on the pipes takes us back to what I said at the beginning of this chapter: All of the problems we face in government today have to do with capacity. People aren't complaining that government isn't developing innovative new services. They aren't returning defective widgets. No, the complaints are that government costs too much, takes too long, and accomplishes too little. These are capacity issues. These are pipe issues. We have to straighten the pipes to speed the flow. Speed the flow, and we will get more done without additional resources.

Our results come from our systems. If you want better results, build better systems. As you will see in the coming chapters, our systems are fundamentally shaped by our beliefs. If we believe all customers are out to game the system, then the system will be designed accordingly. If we believe employees are unskilled, unmotivated, and cannot be trusted, the system will be designed accordingly. To get better results in government, we need to change our systems. To change our systems, we need to change our beliefs.

Better beliefs ➡ Better systems ➡ Better results

So let's turn our attention to those beliefs.

Some of Our Failing Systems

Food Stamps. Over 40 percent of the U.S. population will need Supplemental Nutrition Assistance (as the food stamp program is now called) at some point in their lives. The recent economic collapse sent those numbers through the roof. The recipients of this program aren't freeloaders and welfare queens. They look just like you and me. In fact, the Ford Foundation put up $100 million to improve the system because they realized how many of their auto workers depended on it in tough times. For many, making the decision to enter the benefits office is the hardest pill they've ever had to swallow. They come in hungry and desperate and are told they will get help in thirty days, provided they jump through all the hoops properly.

Bank examinations. Facing growing financial markets without any new resources, bank examiners years ago began lengthening the time between exams. Some banks would go for two years between inspections. How long did it take for the financial industry to collapse?

Adoptions. There are perhaps no pipes as maxed out as the courts and child welfare programs. These pipes are so beyond capacity that they look like a straw in a bucket. Consequently, everyone suffers. The workers who get burned out and blamed, the families involved, and, most importantly, the kids. Typically, if a child is abused and removed from her home, she will bounce around in the pipes for four years before she has a permanent home again.

Immigration. Our country has reached a boiling point regarding immigration. There are a lot of reasons behind the furor, but our dysfunctional systems are exacerbating the problem. The pipes that produce visas, green cards, and passports are completely overwhelmed. There is a strong correlation between ease of compliance and voluntary compliance. When the systems are fast, accessible, and easy to understand, people cooperate — whether it's taxes, child support, or paying parking tickets. When the systems are slow, cumbersome, and unresponsive, people find a different way. All of the laws, constitutional amendments, and border fences will do nothing until our systems have the capacity to meet the citizenship needs of immigrants.

CHAPTER 3
A Mold Epidemic

Mold in a home is an insidious problem. It doesn't explode onto the scene like a busted pipe, or drip drip drip its way into your consciousness like a leaky faucet. People living with mold often don't even know it's in their house. They just know that over time, the family keeps getting sick; they can't breathe well, and a sense of lethargy has taken over. The energy and vitality of the home have slowly turned into chronic illness.

The hallways of government are rife with mold. You can't see it — we've wallpapered over it with vision statements, mission goals, customer-service policies, and employee-of-the-month plaques. But it is there, fouling the air, sickening the family, and destroying the energy and vitality of public service.

How do you know if your agency has a mold problem? Check the symptoms:

- Low morale
- Poor customer service
- CYA
- Silo mentality or turf wars
- Slow processes
- Few innovations or ideas

- Constant complaining
- Apathy
- High absenteeism, grievances, and turnover
- Rampant distrust (of employees, customers, and management)

Just like a family living in a moldy house, the agency becomes lethargic, grey, and chronically ill. There is a subtle, pervasive smell of fear lingering in the carpets, the cubicles, and conference rooms. It's a fear to question. A fear to act. A fear to make a mistake. An outsider (say, a customer) can sense it right away. He sees it in the long lines in the lobby and hears it when told to take a number. It's in the endless posters of policies tacked up on the wall, warning him of what he shouldn't do and reminding him (too late, of course) of everything he forgot to bring with him. The fear is on the face of the frustrated worker who takes all the blame for the policies but lacks any power to change them. The fear sits in every question on the twenty-page form the customer must fill out, the one that culminates in the signature block filled with menacing legal threats.

Everything about the place just screams "no can do" and "you'd better not."

And those are just the visible symptoms.

What outsiders don't see is the mold in the employee break room. (No, I'm not talking about that six-month-old container of curry chicken.) It's the sign that claims "Our employees are our most valued asset" — right next to the thermostat with the lock on it. It's the Employee of the Month wall with a different winner chosen at random every thirty days. It's the poster advertising all the benefits HR can deliver — right next to the bereavement-leave policy underlining in red ink who counts as family. It's the suggestion box located just below the mandatory overtime schedule.

It smells like fear.

Where did the mold come from? From the way we view people. It's the belief that the problems in government are "people problems." That government workers are inferior, or that they're not giving it their all. That they will only do the minimum amount of work required. They can't be trusted and must be controlled, directed, supervised, and inspected.

This view is essentially borne out of what social psychologist Douglas McGregor termed in his 1960 book, *The Human Side of Enterprise,* as the "Theory X" view of people. Theory X holds that people have an inherent dislike of work and will avoid it if they can. They naturally avoid work and shun responsibility. Theory X claims workers are self-centered and do not care about organizational goals and will resist change at all costs.

Of course no one would admit to believing those things. We've become far too enlightened by human resources directors to talk this way. Instead we say this:

> *People are our greatest asset, we just need to develop their competencies and channel their talent toward the pursuit of measurable goals. We need to focus on their strengths, give them positive feedback, and reward and recognize their outstanding performance. We want to motivate them, engage them, and ensure a climate of honesty, openness, and accountability.*

It's the same sentiment with nicer words! Underneath it all is the fundamental belief that we need employees to be more motivated, more engaged, more productive, more accountable. Just *more.* If we could get more from our people we could do more for our citizens. The belief is that we have a people problem. We need you to pedal harder, faster, and in a prescribed direction. When we cling to that belief, we reach for three moldy solutions: Get better people, motivate the ones you have, and hold everyone accountable.

Moldy Solution #1: Get Better People

There is perhaps no better place on earth to view the mold of government than your local DMV. The "no can do" spirit is alive and well on every poster and every face. After an hour in line (and another hour in the wrong line), two more trips, and a migraine, you can't help but scream, "What is wrong with these people?!"

Clearly, it must be a people problem, right?

Well, let's think about that. If we assume it's a people problem, then we are saying that DMV offices nationwide have set out to recruit the grumpiest, slowest, most unsympathetic people they could find. That these employees wake up each day trying to figure out how to aggravate the most people possible with the least amount of effort. That the employees are trying to make each transaction take longer than it should. That the manager of the office is intentionally understaffing the place. That people designed the forms to make them as complex as possible. That people intentionally programmed the computer system to make it hard for employees to find information quickly. That people designing the mailer that reminds you it's time to renew tried their best to obfuscate the information you need behind as much legal language as possible. And that the people who write the policy manuals keep making changes to intentionally confuse the field office staff.

What a grand conspiracy of people all working together to do the worst job possible! And even more dastardly, they have coordinated and replicated this conspiracy nationwide!

It can't be coincidence that all this happened at every DMV in every jurisdiction. Clearly, we need to clean house. Get some new blood in. Even better, let's get some private-sector blood.

Of course now you are faced with the essential "people problem" deal-breaker. If you fired all the people and brought in a whole new crew, how long would it be before you were in the exact same spot?

One of the great "elixirs" sold to the public sector is privatization or outsourcing. In fact, many DMVs have been switched to private ownership with the belief that private-sector folks can do it better, faster, and more cheaply. The result? The same result we saw with privatized food stamp offices, mental health facilities, prisons, and even national defense. The service isn't better or faster, and it's only cheaper for a short while.

Overpromising on Privatization

In the early stages of privatization efforts, the private contractors always bid less than the true cost to perform the function. They then do one of three things:

1) Hire low-cost, low-skilled workers to do what trained professionals used to do. This lowers cost in the short run but raises cost in the long term, as mistakes, shoddy work, and the inability to handle complexity bring these operations to their knees.

2) Make as much of the system dependent on the incumbent vendor and then jack up their price during the next bid cycle, essentially making the cost of switching too high.

3) They simply walk away, admitting what everyone else already knew: You can't make money at this.

So why the continued belief in outsourcing and privatization? Because beneath it is a deeper belief that government workers are somehow defective. That whatever job it may be — from teaching students to inspecting bridges to caring for the elderly — *anybody* can do it better than a government worker. Many people hold this as a universal truth, that private-sector employees are simply better and more

Inside Two Outsourcing Failures

Failure #1: A few years ago, one Midwest state contracted with a tech giant to privatize all its welfare functions. In the deal — worth over $1 billion — the technology firm agreed to manage and process the state's applications for food stamps, Medicaid and other welfare benefits. The effort was plagued by software problems and failed attempts to automate the welfare system. Three years into the agreement, the delays and canceled benefits were so bad that the state asked the company to submit a "corrective action plan." The tech firm came up with a price tag to fix the problems: nearly $200 million more than the initial cost of the deal. The state canceled the agreement and sued for breach of contract. The lawsuit cited such performance failures as "denying Medicaid to a cancer patient because she missed her welfare appointment while hospitalized, denying welfare benefits to a deaf person because she could not do a telephone interview, and a nun who lost Medicaid benefits for being 'uncooperative' when she missed a telephone interview scheduled on a Holy Day and which the nun had requested to be rescheduled." The company, meanwhile, countersued. The lawsuits — and the headaches — are ongoing. (Source: *Outsourcing Insider*, May 18, 2010)

Failure #2: In 2005, a state in the Southwest entered a similar contract for services like food stamps and Medicaid. The five-year, $889 million deal fell apart almost immediately. Call centers weren't equipped to answer applicants' questions, and applicants received inaccurate notices saying they hadn't submitted required paperwork. In 2006, the state reduced the scope of the deal, but the private company wouldn't agree to the new terms. The entire deal was scuttled in 2007. The state still has one of the country's worst rates for getting food stamps to eligible residents, and it's been warned that its entire federal food stamp funds are at risk for failing to improve.

efficient than their public-sector counterparts. (And after corporate America's stellar performance in 2008, who could argue?)

But is this true? Are those of us in government defective in some way? Have all of the slow, inefficient, customer-hating people gravitated to one industry?

Take a moment and think of other industries that you believe struggle as much with customer satisfaction and responsiveness as government does. My workshop participants usually come up with a list that looks like this:

Industries that struggle:

- government
- health care
- utilities
- cable companies
- cell phone providers
- insurance
- education
- banks
- airlines

In today's economy, you can probably think of dozens more. The point is that government is not alone in its struggles. There are plenty of other industries that struggle as much as we do. In fact, when you look at the list, you'll notice that these industries have a few things in common. First, they are all service companies. That is, they are not manufacturing "widgets." That's a little scary, considering the future of our economy is supposed to be "service." We simply haven't learned how to manage service yet. (The secret, of course, as I revealed in *We Don't Make Widgets*, is not to invent a whole new way of managing service, but to think of squishy intangible service work as manufactured widgets, and use the same techniques for making those widgets better, faster, and cheaper.)

The second common aspect of these industries is that there is great confusion about who the customer is. These industries often have multiple customers with competing interests. You're well aware of this conflict in government, especially if you work in a regulatory or compliance agency. But the conflict is not limited to government. For example, who is the customer in health care? Is it the patient? The doctors? The insurance companies? The federal government?

Who is the customer in education? Is it the student? The faculty? Employers? Society? (Or is it even broader? One professor once told me, "My customer is truth." Try managing for *that*.)

But the key thing most of these industries have in common? The reason they're struggling to improve? They're all some form of a monopoly. That is, they have captive customers with little choice. Airlines, government, utilities, schools: They don't have customers. They have hostages.

When customers have no choice, what incentive is there to improve? It's not like they can go somewhere else. That's one thing we've got going for us in government: amazing customer loyalty.

And this is one of the primary arguments for outsourcing government services. Outsourcing advocates believe that using the private sector to provide a service would be better than a public-sector monopoly. The flaw in this logic is that a private-sector monopoly is no better than a public-sector monopoly. The problem is the monopoly itself — the lack of incentive to improve — not who is providing the service.

I have spent many years working with mental health systems. They are a critical government function where people are doing the noblest work in the dreariest pipes. For the longest time, mental health care was the sole provenance of government. Patients were housed in large government-run facilities filled with mold (literally and figuratively). If you're picturing a gloomy place that's dim, grey, and devoid of spirit, you're not far off, at least based on the wards I have visited.

Again, the mold was sensed most easily by outsiders, specifically the families of the patients. They felt their loved ones were not getting the quality of care that they deserved. There was a widespread belief that these government workers lacked compassion and didn't care about patient well-being. The solution? Privatization, of course. Because private workers trying to turn a profit are obviously more compassionate than public employees trying to make a difference.

What sprang up was a collection of private mental health providers nationwide. There is no doubt the addition of these providers has been tremendously helpful in handling the capacity crunch in the mental health system. But did the care improve?

I had the opportunity to lead focus groups with families of mental health patients who were in private facilities. What do you suppose was still their No. 1 complaint? Quality of care. In their words, "The staff lacks empathy and compassion. They don't care about the well-being of the patients and aren't listening to what we want." How could this be? These were private-sector employees, genetically superior to their public-sector counterparts. How could the performance be exactly the same? It's simple, of course: The funding source was the same. The quality of care was not a function of who was performing the tasks — public or private — but who paid the bills. In this case, that meant the legislature.

The large public mental health hospitals were funded by state legislatures. This meant that to secure funding, facility administrators just had to keep the legislature happy. The patients weren't funding their care, nor were the families. Hence they felt powerless, and indeed they were. They were hostages: No choice, no voice. It's no surprise that the institutions felt like prisons. But when the time came to privatize the care, where did the new mental health providers get their money from? The same source: the legislature. In effect, the legislatures had just created private-sector monopolies.

How did the mental health system finally resolve this decades-long conundrum? In some places throughout the country, courageous groups of activists, patient advocates, and mental health professionals have pushed for a change. In those places, the money for mental health treatment is bypassing the government agencies and private providers and being given directly to the families. The families get to decide what care they want and who provides it. They have the power. Now, the agencies and providers have to make *them* happy in order to secure *their* funding. The whole system has been turned upside down. The result? Families and patients are happier and providers are continuously improving. And believe it or not, costs have gone down. Study after study has shown that when the families have control of the money, they spend more discriminately and end up spending less per patient than before.

This same scene is playing out in school choice movements throughout the nation. Again, public-sector teachers and administrators are being vilified and told that they are the problem and the only solution is to have someone else teach the children. And again, charter schools and private providers who get their money

When Privatization Works

There are definitely times when turning to the private sector is a good idea. The expertise required for a job may be too rare and too costly to develop in-house. Or maybe there simply isn't enough capacity inside the agency to keep up. Good examples include using private collection agencies for outstanding fees and taxes, or employing private after-hours child-abuse investigation units.

from the same source with the same strings attached experience the exact same challenges. It is when money (and choice) is given to parents that major system change starts to happen. Again, it's not genetics; it's finances. Most of the private providers are staffed with former public-school professionals. But to secure funding, the providers in a choice environment have to keep families happy — not boards, taxpayers, or agencies.

Private-sector monopolies are no better than public-sector ones. Private-sector monopolies brought us the beige telephone, Power-Point and "We will install your cable between the hours of 9 a.m. and next Wednesday." The only difference between an AT&T store and a DMV is color scheme. Do you actually think corporate employees like their HR or IT departments any more than you do? It's the lack of competition and customer choice that are the source of the dysfunction — not whether a service is provided for profit or not.

Moldy Solution #2: Motivate the People You Have

Motivation seems to be as American as apple pie and Coca-Cola. There are volumes of books written about it. Every champion coach or Hall of Fame player has a book on it. We have this great American ideal that somehow we can take a ragtag bunch of misfits in Chico's Bail Bonds uniforms and motivate them to win the big championship game. With the right speech, the right pat on the back, or the right kick in the backside, we can help those crazy kids excel beyond their wildest dreams.

Motivation is the fuel of the great American work ethic. And so we believe that this magic fuel should work equally as well in the workplace. We read the great books from the legendary basketball coach or buy the tapes from the big-toothed grinning guy on TV and learn about focusing and setting goals and overcoming obstacles. And we bring all that stuff back to the cubicles hoping that once again we can help this bunch rise up. Well, all those books and tapes should come with a warning label: "Please apply to yourself only. The following techniques won't work on anybody else. Or if they do, it'll only be for a short while." You see, there's one nagging secret about motivation that, if it ever got out, would end the entire industry in a heartbeat: You cannot motivate someone.

Let me illustrate with a story about my daughter's room. It's constantly a mess. I don't just mean your typical pre-teen messy room. We're talking messes of epic proportion. Messes that start in her room, extend down the hallway, and eventually creep down the stairs. Whenever a piece of apparel finally snakes its way all the way to the kitchen, my wife freaks out and quarantines the house until the situation is resolved. Same pattern, month after month. As loving parents, we care very much for our daughter's creativity and her individuality and her desire to express herself. But we'd also rather not live under a mountain of filth. So, using all of the motivational techniques that my wife and I have learned through the countless workshops we've attended throughout our professional lives, we set about trying to inspire greatness in cleanliness from our daughter.

We began with an inspirational talk about how mommy and daddy would greatly desire to live in a home where we are not tripping over piles of clothes. She nodded her head and our message really seemed to resonate. We were so proud! And then she proceeded to continue the behaviors as before. So, on to Plan B: Pay for Performance. You clean up your room, you get a reward. We also created an accountability system to go with this. It wasn't a full-on balanced scorecard or dashboard, but we did have a magnetic board with the days of the week and a little check mark if tasks were accomplished. If she cleaned her room three out of five days, she was eligible for the reward of her choice. Now, on Day One, we made a big deal about this. We had the initiative kick-off — unveiling the big board, showcasing the rewards, and getting her "buy-in" to the big program. And on Day One she actually cleaned her room. It was quite amazing, and my wife and I both went to sleep with great big smiles on our faces. We had accomplished what the motivational speakers had told us! We had set a goal, held her accountable, given instantaneous feedback and positive reinforcement. We were textbook awesome.

De-motivation

What I truly learned from trying to motivate our daughter was the effect it had on our other child. My son is naturally neat. He cleans his room regularly because he likes a clean room. Suddenly, once we started this pay-for-performance scheme with our daughter, he stopped cleaning his room. I asked him why. He looked at me and asked, "What will you give me if I clean it?"

Day Two went very much like Day One. We did the same things — positive reinforcement, reminders about the great rewards available. And that day went pretty much the same. But on Day Three, we became a little distracted, and sure enough, as bedtime approached, my daughter hadn't cleaned her room. So we kicked into accountability mode: More speechmaking, more incentivizing. And with considerably more effort, we were able to get the room clean on Day Three. On Day Four, we totally forgot about it. And she did too. And then again on Day Five and Day Six. And the mess, of course, began to pile up all over again.

At that point, like all good managers, we first blamed ourselves. We hadn't followed through. We hadn't stuck to the system. Maybe the big board was too complicated? Or maybe we needed to put it on the computer or build in a regular meeting time each morning to discuss our daughter's progress? We redoubled our efforts, including, yes, instituting a regular meeting to talk about the room. Again, things went well for several days. It really seemed like our daughter was motivated to clean her room. But as soon as we stopped focusing on it, she stopped focusing on it. And after a month of beating ourselves up about our inability to stick with the program, and another month questioning whether our child had any motivation (or hygiene) whatsoever, we shifted to Plan C: Punishment. You don't clean your room, you don't get to go outside. You don't get to have friends over. And again we got compliance.

Now, in this whole scenario, who was motivated? Who expended all the effort? What my wife and I were doing is so similar to what all the managers and supervisors and department heads are doing in agencies across the country. *We* were the ones with the goal. *We* were the ones expending energy. The systems we created were *ours*.

What this example points out (besides our ineffective parenting) is the difference between motivation and movement. Movement is about compliance. It's about doing the minimum work it takes to avoid punishment. Motivation, on the other hand, is about energy. It can come from two sources: inside (intrinsic) or outside (extrinsic). Intrinsic motivation is a limitless energy source. Extrinsic motivation, positive or negative, is limited. You only get out of someone what you put into them. The energy to move them comes from you. You are motivated; they are moved. Obviously, intrinsic motivation is the preferable energy source.

The most common extrinsic mover is money. One of the things we've seen in government over the past decade is the rise of pay-for-performance programs. These programs come to us courtesy of the private sector. Great titans of industry have written large volumes about how they turned around whole corporations using these pay-for-performance motivational systems. And, as government is wont to do with just about every private-sector initiative, we imported it to the public sector about a decade later.

Like many of the traditional motivational tactics, pay-for-performance has largely gone unchallenged as an effective means of increasing performance. Again corresponding to that great American work ethic, it's the belief that if you work harder you should get rewarded. Hence, greater rewards will yield more hard work. What could possibly be wrong with that?

In truth, there are some very deep, unchallenged assumptions behind pay-for-performance. The first is the notion that you aren't already working as hard as you can. Up until now, you've been withholding a certain amount of effort; you haven't been fully committing. But maybe if we dangle the right incentive in front of you, you'll suddenly kick into high gear. I'm always amazed by this idea, because the people that I know who work in government tend to sleep with two BlackBerrys under their pillow. Now, are there people who perhaps aren't pedaling as hard as everybody else? Of course. But they are a very small minority.

The second bold assumption of a pay-for-performance approach is that you can actually separate a given individual's performance from the system itself, or from the collective contribution of everyone else. We talk all the time about teamwork, yet when it comes time to motivate or incentivize, we act as if the only thing that matters is the individual contribution of singular employees. We can't have it both ways.

Culture Shock

The most common thing I hear from private-sector execs who do a tour of duty in the public sector: "I have been really surprised by how hard everyone works."

The reality is that employees, as hard as they may work, will always eventually bump up against some kind of system constraint. An employee's individual performance isn't necessarily indicative of her contribution.

The third and perhaps biggest assumption of pay-for-performance is that money is, in fact, a motivator. Of course there's no question that money's important. I like money as much as the next guy. But is money truly a motivator of great performance? The current research confirms what my workshop participants have been telling me for years: Simply, money can be a de-motivator, but it's not a motivator. It can be a mover. No question about that. We can use money to push and pull people in different directions. But again, all the energy is coming from the managers, the ones dangling the carrot. Even as a mover, money's not all that effective. Research continues to show that you can move someone once, twice, maybe three times with a monetary incentive. If you want more, you're going to have to boost the amount you're offering, and the frequency. That means more energy expended by you for diminishing returns from the person you're trying to move.

And here's a shocking fact: People don't go into public-sector work in order to get rich. Research on public-sector employees shows that money is not a driving factor in their satisfaction. It's usually ranked somewhere around sixth or seventh. What is No. 1 on that list? Making a difference. Having an impact and feeling like you're contributing to something bigger than yourself. So every time we try to motivate an employee with money, we're appealing to No. 7 on the list of what's important to them.

Want an open-and-shut case against the efficacy of pay-for-performance plans? Just look at what's happened in the latest fiscal crisis. Facing staggering budget shortfalls, nearly every one of the pioneering governments with pay-for-performance programs has had to eliminate the "pay" part. They still have all the same goals, measures, and paperwork. There's just no pot of gold at the end of the rainbow anymore. And what has happened to performance? Interestingly, nothing. Employees are still serving just as many customers and still finding just as many innovative ways to contribute to their communities. Taking the money away hasn't decreased their motivation, because offering it never increased their motivation in the first place.

As with nearly all individual performance initiatives, the cure ends up being more harmful than the disease. So why do we keep doing it? Again, it comes back to fairness. We have a well-intentioned desire to reward those who seem to be above and beyond everyone else. But 85 percent of your workforce thinks they are those people. When you hear employees talk about their dissatisfaction with the pay system, typically what they are reacting to is the perception of fairness. Or put another way, "I cannot believe that guy's making as much as I am." It's more a reflection of our inability to deal with poor performers. In fact, I've been doing a little informal research for the past decade. In my workshops, I've asked thousands of managers, "If you were given a choice between a two-step pay increase, which in your jurisdiction may be a 3 to 5 percent pay bump, or the organization finally doing something about the poor performers, which would you choose?" Nearly unanimously, they say they'd rather do something about the dead wood. Find a way to deal with poor performers: Identify them and either improve their performance or move them out of the organization. If we would do that, then we wouldn't have to do all the other things we do in an effort to reward everybody else. Rather than punishing the entire organization with de-motivating pay-for-performance and incentive schemes, we could simplify everything by focusing our attention on dealing with those poor performers.

Pay-for-performance, monetary incentives, piecemeal bonuses — they're holdovers from the Industrial Age, when we were all making widgets. A time when we were cranking the same wrench or tightening the same lug nuts over and over, day after day. Workers were hands, not brains. And getting hands to do more work often requires a great expense of energy through monetary incentives to get higher performance. We don't make widgets anymore. This is the Information Age. We produce things with our minds, not our hands. And to use our minds to the fullest, we need to look at problems in their broadest sense. We need to deal with complexity, ambiguity, and variety. You can't fit most of today's problems into small incentivized boxes.

The Cruelty Curve

What is absolutely tragic to watch with so many of these pay-for-performance initiatives is what occurs when the system starts to mature — especially when the organization runs into tough budget times. Fiscal cutbacks force executives to limit the number of people who can receive any kind of award. So they implement a bell curve. Say you have ten employees: Now, only two of them can receive an outstanding rating. Six can be rated in the middle categories and two need to be in the bottom part of the distribution. This is a great misreading of statistical probability, to assume that every single work unit is a perfect natural distribution of employees. Maybe if your ten employees all performed the exact same tasks day in and day out, there might be a way to fit their performance into a bell curve. But even then, what if they're universally fantastic performers? This whole system is incredibly problematic in a world where 85 percent of people view themselves as above average. In our well-intentioned attempts to reward our great performers, we are in fact creating a system that is de-motivating *all* the performers.

Moldy Thinking #3: Hold 'Em Accountable

Every candidate running for office pledges two things: to crack down on waste, fraud, and abuse, and to hold people accountable. It sounds like leadership. But it smells like mold.

The accountability systems we've come to associate with good management are actually creating chronic illness by poisoning government with toxic mold. These systems are based on the belief that good performance comes from holding people accountable for achieving measurable goals. This belief manifests itself it in the measurement systems, dashboards, scorecards, performance management, and STAT sessions that permeate government today. Measure performance, set a goal, and hold people accountable for achieving it. That's great leadership, right? Let's give it some more thought.

My view on accountability was greatly changed by the stories of soldiers from World War II. My grandfather had fought in the war, but, like so many of his generation, had chosen not to speak of it. I had no idea what he went through until I saw the incredible work of Stephen Ambrose, Steven Spielberg, and Tom Hanks in the HBO mini-series *Band of Brothers*. This graphic, eye-popping series followed Easy Company from the storming of Normandy Beach through the liberation and the eventual end of the European conflict. Each episode of the ten-part series showed a key battle through the eyes of one of the true-life characters. You saw what they saw and felt what they felt through some amazing acting and directorial magic. What was most memorable, however, were the final five minutes of each story, when the show interviewed the actual soldier depicted. Seeing the gentleness in their faces and the wisdom in their eyes, the bottled-up pain and their lifelong quest for a peaceful place to live out their days, brought me to tears. I appreciated my grandfather as I never had before.

If you've seen the series or know about the events, you know that these men displayed acts of unthinkable courage. They ran head-long into a hail of bullets. They dived on grenades and ran across enemy lines with little regard for their own life. How? How did the military breed that kind of dedication? How do they continue to do that? Why does a soldier give his life? Surely it's because he is accountable to his Sergeant and doesn't want to let his Sergeant down. And the Sergeant is accountable to his Major, and the Major to his Colonel. And all the way up the chain, everybody is accountable to someone above them. Right?

What the military knows, and what the soldiers in *Band of Brothers* revealed, was exactly the opposite. They didn't feel accountable to their commanding officer. Heck, they didn't even like their commanding officer and couldn't care less about *his* commanding officer. They were accountable to each other. They would rather take a bullet than see their friend take one. They risked their lives to save the man next to them, knowing full well that man would do the same. True accountability is shoulder-to-shoulder. It's horizontal. Yet we keep trying to make it vertical. True accountability looks like love; we keep making it feel like fear.

Rather than creating a band of brothers (and sisters), rather than cultivating teamwork, togetherness and — dare I say it? — love, we continue to divide, separate, and force competition. We incentivize the chain of command but do little to cultivate the foxhole. Accountability is fear's slightly more attractive cousin. Fear does not breed excellence. Fear will make me do just enough to not get fired.

Management-by-fear is the current fad. Again, nobody calls it that. But across the country, in conference rooms of every size, governors are looking at cabinet members' performance measures and demanding to know why the curve isn't bending. There are city managers berating department heads because the trend line is going in the wrong direction. There are federal appointees making up excuses for why the green light turned yellow on their dashboard. Again, I understand why these are attractive programs. I used to design and sell them myself. They feel like they're the right thing to do. Unfortunately, not only are they doomed to fail, they produce devastating side effects.

The first side effect is the accountability trap. The conversation goes something like this:

> Manager: "We need to hold you accountable for a measurable goal."
>
> Worker: "You can't measure what I do."
>
> Manager: "Well, we have to measure *something*."
>
> Worker: "We can measure how many things I do."
>
> Manager: "I don't care how many things you do. I care about what results you are achieving."
>
> Worker: "Our results don't show up every quarter. We may not know for years what impact we are having."
>
> Manager: "The accountability sessions are every quarter. We need a chart every quarter."
>
> Worker: "We can measure how many we produce every quarter."
>
> Manager: "Fine. Let's start there."

Flash forward to the first review meeting, as they look at the chart showing the amount of volume produced:

> Manager: "It seems like you guys aren't producing as much as last quarter."
>
> Worker: "It fluctuates quarter to quarter. Nothing to worry about."
>
> Manager: "Well, I need an explanation."

Worker: "I thought you didn't care about how many we produce."

Manager: "I don't. But my boss cares about how many of my measures are going the wrong direction."

Worker: "Tell him it doesn't matter. We care about results, and those take time. The volume isn't important."

Manager: "I will tell him that you are working on a corrective action plan and that volume will be up next quarter."

Game the System! STAT!
excerpted from *the New York Times*

"SECRET TAPE HAS POLICE PRESSING TICKET QUOTAS"
By Al Baker and Ray Rivera
Sept. 9, 2010

No matter how often the Police Department denies the existence of quotas, many New Yorkers will swear that officers are sometimes forced to write a certain number of tickets in a certain amount of time.

Now, in a secret recording made in a police station in Brooklyn, there is persuasive evidence of the existence of quotas.

The hourlong recording, which a lawyer provided this week to *The New York Times*, was made by a police supervisor during a meeting in April of supervisors from the 81st Precinct.

The recording makes clear that precinct leaders were focused on raising the number of summonses issued — even as the Police Department had already begun an inquiry into whether crime statistics in that precinct were being manipulated.

And that's the trap. We want to hold someone accountable for results. We want it to be objective, measurable. Results are hard to measure, but we feel like we have to measure something. So we measure what's easy, rather than what's important. What gets measured gets done, so we have just shifted the focus to what is unimportant and easy to measure. In most of the conference rooms I have visited, managers are conducting fearful interrogations with powerless people over inconsequential things that are easy to measure, instead of inquisitive dialogues among peers

---

The Police Department's chief spokesman, Paul J. Browne, did not respond Thursday to three e-mails and three phone calls requesting comments on the tape. He was sent extensive excerpts from the recording.

On the tape, a police captain, Alex Perez, can be heard warning his top commanders that their officers must start writing more summonses or face consequences. Captain Perez offered a precise number and suggested a method. He said each officer on a day tour should write 20 summonses a week: five each for double-parking, parking at a bus stop, driving without a seat belt and driving while using a cell phone.

"You, as bosses, have to demand this and have to count it," Captain Perez said, citing pressure from top police officials. At another point, Captain Perez emphasized his willingness to punish officers who do not meet the targets, saying, "I really don't have a problem firing people."

Critics say this is the flip side of CompStat, the Police Department analysis system that has been credited with bringing down major crimes but faulted as creating a numbers-driven culture.

about important things that may be hard to measure.

Managing for results seems intrinsically like the right thing to do. Indeed, we absolutely should focus on results, track whether we're impacting those results and evaluate our strategies. The problems arise when we go from *focusing* on results to holding people *accountable* for them.

To see how the problems are created, one need look no further than the ubiquitous surveys that are thrust upon us after every visit to a restaurant, hospital, or even church service. I mentioned this in the *Widgets* book and have since had my inbox flooded with stories from readers who had the same experience I did: Their car salesman, waitress, and even nurse handed them a satisfaction survey — already filled out with perfect scores. Rather than being a tool to learn from customers, these surveys have become an instrument for banging people over the head. These people game the system to avoid the hammer. It's a perfectly rational reaction: the smart choice when faced with being held personally accountable for a broken system is to game the measurement system.

Whenever we use measurement as anything other than a learning tool, we're just asking for employees to game the system. Measurement should help us ask *why?*, not *who?* It should help raise questions, not lower the boom.

Let me give you an example from my own box of mistakes. One of my favorite jobs ever was overseeing 168 DMV offices. Working with the employees and management, we accomplished a lot of great things. The performance measurement system wasn't one of them. Our goal was to hold each office accountable for meeting customer-desired targets of shorter wait times (ten minutes or less) and fewer repeat visits. Each office went through a timing exercise once a month at the busiest hours of the busiest day. Using time stamps, we knew when the customers came in, when they got to the counter, and when they left. Each month, the office managers would gather together to show us their charts.

In the first month, one office reported customer wait times of twenty minutes. We asked lots of questions of the manager, but she had very few answers. Our reply to her was something along the lines of, "It's one thing to miss the target; it's another not to know why. 'I don't know' isn't good enough."

A month later, the office manager came back and reported that wait times were down to ten minutes. We showered her with praise and asked how she'd done it. But again, she didn't know. Our reply was something along the lines of, "It's great that you hit the target, but we're concerned that you don't know why. 'I don't know' isn't good enough."

The next month, her times were back up — way up. Over thirty minutes. We asked her why, and this time she had a theory. "Perhaps all the praise we got last month caused the workers to relax a bit. I'll make sure they keep their focus."

The following month, wait times were back down to near ten minutes. What had she done? "I stayed on top of them like I said I would." Great, we told her. Keep up the good work.

The month after that, wait times went back up again. What had happened? She had a laundry list of reasons: Marge was on maternity leave, the computers were slow, and there was an extra Monday in the month. Having read a recent book on positive reinforcement, I suggested that she try hard all month to spot people doing good work and praise them. She agreed to try.

The next month, wait times went down a little bit. I felt like a genius. We told her to keep up the positive reinforcement.

Next month? Wait times were the worst ever, a fact the manager was all too quick to let me know. "I told you that touchy-feely stuff doesn't work," she told us. "You gotta give 'em a swift kick in the backside if you want any results."

The office manager administered a kickin', and, sure enough, performance improved. I was dumbfounded. That's not how you are supposed to manage! Fortunately for my ego, the next two months under her iron fist were two of the worst months in the office's history.

We were stuck. Everything appeared to work and not to work. I was completely stumped — until I learned the secret of variation. I had to read in a book what my kids sing all the time: "What goes up must come down."

Why did wait times go up this month? Probably because they were down last month. Why were they down last month? Because they were up the month before. All performance varies around a mean. That is, over time, performance will achieve an average level — say, twenty-minute wait times. But any given data point will likely be above or below that average. If it's above the average one month, it is likely to be below it the next month or the month after that. That is statistics. And there's no point arguing with statistics — which is exactly what we'd been doing.

The performance of any system varies around a mean. Some systems have a wide variance, such as wait times that vary between ten minutes and forty-five minutes on a twenty-minute average. Other ranges can be quite narrow: The average point guard in the NBA is 6'3" tall. A few are 6'7" and some are 6 feet, but you don't see many 5- or 7-foot-tall point guards. There will always be a variance. The source of that variance is the fundamental concept government continues to overlook.

We tend to view all variance as man-made. That is, that all variance has a cause and hence someone to blame. The reality is that variance has two causes. In statistical parlance, these are called common-cause variations and special-cause variations. Common-cause refers to the typical, historical, quantifiable variation within a system. The variance is inside the system: There is no assignable cause. Special-cause variations, on the other hand, refer to unusual anomalies that haven't previously been observed. Something outside the system has caused the performance variance. It's a surprise.

Let's go back to my DMV example. The two types of variances are best understood when looking at a chart of DMV wait times. We are going to add three lines: the mean, the upper limit, and the lower limit.

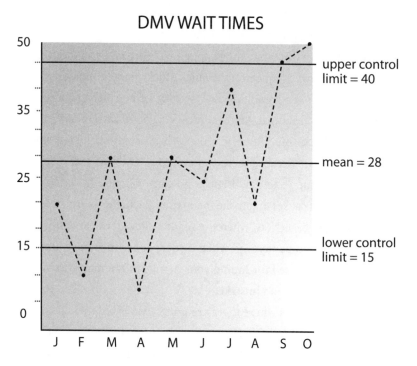

DMV WAIT TIMES

upper control limit = 40

mean = 28

lower control limit = 15

J F M A M J J A S O

Any data points inside the limits are common-cause variations. There is no cause because there are millions of causes. There is as much probability of a data point being at twenty-five minutes as thirty-five minutes. You will notice that only a few data points fell outside this range. That would be special-cause variation. Something happened. There was an actual cause and we should try to figure out what it was so we can learn from it. (Same goes for the data points that fall below the lower limit: Something good happened, and maybe we can learn something positive.)

When you don't understand variation, and specifically the difference between the two types, you make three monumental, morale-killing (mold-spreading) mistakes:

1. Looking for answers when there are none. When we don't understand the concept of common-cause variation, we wind up badgering our managers to explain perfectly natural events. And, behaving completely rationally, they make stuff up. They have to; there is no answer. You see this same thing happening every night on the evening news. They always squeeze in a quick stock-market update — "The Dow is down twenty points today" — with a completely made-up explanation "on fears that Aerosmith may have to cancel their Middle East Comeback Tour." Reporters always have a reason and it is always made up. Why? Because there is no reason. It's down today because it was up a little yesterday. There is no cause because there are literally billions of causes that make the market fluctuate. To isolate one is misleading at best. Now, when the market slides far below the lower limit, it's time to panic. And when it soars above the upper limit, it's time to kick yourself for hiding your money in the mattress. Which leads me to the second mistake.

2. Seeing trends where there are none. Two bad days in the stock market is not a trend. Three games without a hit is not a trend. Statistics show that in order to accurately determine a trend you need thirteen data points. Thirteen! This is why most performance measurement/accountability initiatives are at best a waste of time, and at worst an infestation of mold. Two data points do not equal a trend! But management doesn't have the patience to wait. If you capture data monthly, it'll be more than a year before you can establish a trend (provided there are no seasonal fluctuations). If you capture data quarterly, you won't be able to see a trend for more than three years. Who can wait that long? The leadership will be gone before the trend is established. So they don't wait. They pounce on any apparent trend they can find. Which leads to the third killer mistake.

3. Finding heroes and villains when there are neither. When the data goes up we want to throw a pizza party. When it goes down we want to kick some butt. Both reactions are wrong. If the variation is common-cause, inside the system, then the change in data is pure luck. How would you feel getting a reward for something you didn't do? How about getting punished for something you didn't do?

As I mentioned, I learned all this the hard way. After uncovering the hidden-in-plain-sight secret of variation, I went back and talked to several of the DMV managers. I asked them, "When we wanted explanations for your results, were you just making stuff up?" Yep, they replied. "And the pizza parties we threw to celebrate the good months, you had no idea what you did right?" Nope, they told me: "Chalked it up to good luck. Enjoyed the pizza, though."

The reality was that there was rarely a special cause for the changes in DMV wait times. Rather, it was the random interaction of countless variables — the weather, the day of the week, the month of the year, how many cars parked in the lot at once, and so on. Occasionally, we could point to special causes — the network went down for a day, an office underwent mass staff turnover, a new law was passed that drove up traffic for a time. In most cases, though, we knew those causes long before the data came in.

We have done an amazing job training government managers on how to develop performance measures. What we haven't done is train their bosses how to use performance data. We need a nationwide performance measurement safety class so no one else gets hurt.

Common-cause variation is not a reason to give up on improving performance. If your goal is to reduce DMV wait times to ten minutes, and the wait time for one month comes in at thirty-five minutes, I'm not saying it's okay to shrug your shoulders and say, "Well, it's within the upper limit, so I guess it's good enough." The best outcome would be performance that is invariably awesome. But how do we do that? Change the system. Accountability doesn't change the system. Yelling at the system doesn't change the system. Stretch targets don't change the system. The only thing that changes the system is changing the system. Everything else is just spreading the mold.

The Problem with Stretching

Stretch targets are a complete waste of time. As the statistician W. Edwards Deming taught us, a system is perfectly designed to achieve the results it achieves. What you get is what you get. The only way you will get a different level of performance is to actually fix the system. Wishing won't make it so. Want better results? Build a better system.

Once you build a better system, what good was the arbitrary target? The new system will produce exactly what it is going to produce. No more, no less. Why constrain the thinking by setting a target? As we will discuss in Chapter 6, there is a chance to reduce time by over 80 percent, capacity by 40 percent, and quality by at least 50 percent. None of those things will be achieved if we have arbitrary 3, 5, or 10 percent goals. The system will produce what the system will produce. Instead of an arbitrary target, the only goal should be to maximize the performance of the system — period. Do everything in your power to remake the system better, faster, and cheaper, and then continuously improve it to squeeze out every last drop you can. That is the purpose of the rest of this book.

CHAPTER 4

Eradicating the Mold

When was the last time you had a TGIM moment?

Seriously, when was the last time you thought, "Thank God it's Monday"? The last time you said, "I'm so glad the weekend is over so that I can finally do what I really want to be doing — work."

Most people laugh when I ask that in my workshops. But I bet you remember a time when you actually *have* had a TGIM moment, a time when you looked forward to getting to work, and time on the job seemed to fly by. What made you feel that way? Here's what some public-sector workers have told me:

- I believed I was making a difference.
- I could see the impact of my work.
- I felt challenged.
- I was learning a new skill.
- I worked with great people to achieve something impossible.
- I helped someone.

Guess what never shows up on that list? I got a bonus.

As I said in Chapter 3, blaming the problems of government on public servants creates a breeding ground for mold. Motivating someone extrinsically is inefficient, and pay-for-performance schemes only exacerbate the problems and take the focus off the kinked-up pipes.

But there are ways to drive engagement, passion, and commitment. There are ways to boost employees' satisfaction and create an environment where public servants can't wait to get to work. There are ways to make TGIM moments happen every day.

In his book *Drive: The Surprising Truth About What Motivates Us*, management author Dan Pink lists three easy-to-remember drivers of employee engagement: Mastery, autonomy, and purpose. Let's take a close look at each one of those.

Mastery. Anyone who plays golf, poker, chess, or any other game of skill knows about mastery. It's that incredible feeling you get when you conquer something (or someone), or when you feel your skill level rising. It's also that feeling you get when your skill plateaus and you're energized to break through the next performance barrier. Mastery is what keeps me at the driving range when the staff all wants to go home. I don't get a prize for all the golf balls I hit, and I certainly am not getting paid for it. (I'd have to win two major championships to break even at this point.) The challenge is its own reward.

If you've left your house in the past three years, you've seen someone working a Sudoku puzzle. I was on a flight recently, sitting next to a woman with a Sudoku book so big she had to pay a baggage fee to bring it on. After an hour or so of watching her tear through the puzzles, I finally asked her, "Excuse me, why do you do that? What do you get when you finish the puzzle or the whole book?"

She looked at me with total joy and said, "I get to do another one."

Now, in the moldy worldview where people dislike work and only do something if they are praised, rewarded, and "motivated," her answer makes no sense. She is doing hard work (Knowledge Age hard work, not Widget Age hard work) for nothing more than a sense of personal satisfaction. Again, the challenge is its own reward.

This phenomenon was best explained by positive psychologist Mihály Csíkszentmihályi.

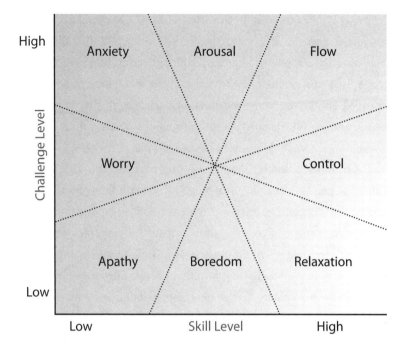

As you can see in Csíkszentmihályi's illustration, when both your skill level and your challenge level are high, you enter the flow state. High skills and low challenges yield boredom. Low skills and high challenges breed anxiety. But when we hit that sweet spot, when the challenge is slightly higher than our skill level, we are in flow — that magic experience in which time stands still and joy is accelerated.

For example, I like to play tennis. I'm a recreational player and can hold my own against most other recreational players. If I were suddenly thrust into a match against Roger Federer for the deed to my house, I would be in a state of complete anxiety. Roger, on the other hand, would be in a state of complete boredom. (He'd also be the proud new owner of a home in sunny Kansas City.) But when I play tennis against someone slightly better than I am, the challenge raises my skill level and I'm totally enthralled in the experience. We see this all the time in sports. A team plays up or down to the level of its competition.

What is it like to be in the flow state? It's a TGIM moment. You are energized, engaged, and want to be doing nothing else other than this. You work harder, practice harder, and look forward to the next challenge. Isn't this exactly what we want in the workplace? If you want engaged employees, you need flow. Mission statements, suggestion boxes, and logo shirts don't create engagement. Mastery does.

So how do we build mastery in the workplace? It's not something you can do corporately. There is no program you can kick off, no catchy slogan you can put on a mug. To increase flow and mastery, you have to continue to find ways to help employees move along both axes — skills and challenges — simultaneously. If you train your staff but don't give them any new challenges in which to apply those new skills, you're merely increasing boredom. If you introduce new challenges to the workplace, such as new responsibilities or a new system to be learned, without simultaneously raising employee skill levels, you're only increasing anxiety. It's a delicate balance. It's the leader's challenge.

Autonomy. Autonomy is freedom. In its extreme, it's what every teenager dreams of: doing whatever you want, whenever you want, without answering to anybody. (At least, that's what my teenage kid dreams of.) Obviously, we have important rules and regulations in the public sector, so total autonomy isn't realistic. But any freedoms added to an oppressive environment can make a world of difference. (Think of the cold beer on the rooftop in *The Shawshank Redemption*.)

What can we do in the public sector to create more autonomy for our workforce? Find out what an employee is passionate about and give her the time to pursue it. This goes hand-in-hand with mastery. I'm reminded of one of my first office assistants. She was exceptionally bright and loved computers, but she had no education beyond high school. It was pretty clear which things she liked doing for me (anything that involved a computer) and those she didn't (anything that involved finding something on my desk). So I continued to give her more and more computer-related projects, each more challenging than before. She would work like crazy to master a new piece of software and would exceed my expectations every time. She really took to graphic layouts and Web design. Before long, word got out about her skills, and other people came to her for help. It was a joy watching her develop on the job. And even though she wasn't working just on my stuff, she got everything done and was as engaged an employee as I'd ever seen. Sadly, when I moved on to another job, her new boss pulled the plug on her side projects — and her motivation.

Autonomy will come to the public-sector workplace, it will just take time. Organized efforts such as ROWE (Results-Oriented Work Environment), in which employees work from home and set their own hours, are already showing very positive results in a handful of government workplaces. Eventually, it will be the norm. Newer generations of workers — synced to the cloud, Skyping and tweeting all day — will simply not tolerate being chained to a cubicle or punching a clock. They are an amazingly productive generation; they just don't fit the 8-to-5 world that we have codified.

Purpose. This is where we have a tremendous advantage over the private sector. Research into employee engagement has revealed a near universal desire for people to feel like their life's work has made a difference. They want to know that they didn't just give forty years of their life for a paycheck. Rather, they want to feel that they've made an impact. This ethic is especially high among the younger generations who are eschewing corporate careers and choosing instead to work with nonprofits.

Purpose-driven careers are the public sector's ace in the hole. How are we not seizing on this?

Watching the private sector try to create purpose is almost comical. I remember sitting through a management retreat where a private-sector consultant was teaching us how to create mission statements. He was so animated, especially when he mentioned PepsiCo. He shouted, "Pepsi's mission is two words: Beat Coke!" Wow, you spent your precious time on this earth selling more sugar water than the other guys. How very inspiring.

Any attempts by corporate America to create purpose are contrived and artificial. Their purpose is to make money, now and in the future. That's not a personal judgment; it's simply their role. They exist to maximize the return to their investors. And what the investors want is money.

The public sector is also called on to maximize return to investors. But our investors don't want money. They invest in us for far more important reasons: to protect children, ensure freedom, provide economic opportunity, protect the environment, rehabilitate offenders, and on and on. This is our profit, our bottom line.

In my career, I've often been able to accompany government employees on "ride-arounds" to better understand what they do. These have been some of the most rewarding times I've spent in government. Employees' faces light up when they recount stories of the impact they have had on people's lives. There was the ride-around with the child protective worker who proudly pointed out various houses where there had been issues as she talked about what a tremendous impact her agency had had in reducing chronic child neglect. There was the ride-around with the environmental workers as they pointed to an area that previously was an ecological disaster but was now thriving, thanks to their partnership with industry to find new solutions. I've been with economic developers who have shown me community revitalizations and anti-poverty workers whose cubicles were wallpapered with snapshots of the families they'd helped get back on their feet.

Everyone — from district managers and file clerks to administrative staff and field workers — should have the opportunity to touch and see the impact being made by their agency. They should get a chance to meet the people who have been helped, see the neighborhood that's thriving, or hear from the families whose loved ones were safeguarded. Private-sector companies engage in "profit-sharing" to give employees a stake in the success of the business and motivate everyone around a common goal. Our "profit-sharing" can do the same things, and so much more. In the private sector, profit-sharing is limited to cash or stocks. While cash may make a great reward, it's a terrible gift. (Ever give your sweetheart cash for Valentine's Day?) We have the opportunity in the public sector, by ensuring our people can see and feel the impact of their work, to give our employees a gift — something they will remember.

As you can see, motivation is not easy. We can't buy a few posters and hand out some logo pens. No speech or book is going to create an energized and engaged workforce. Rather, we must recognize that motivation flows from within. While we can strive to create environments where mastery, autonomy, and purpose thrive, our best course of action is often to simply remove the things that get in the way of self-motivation. Our job is to eradicate the mold so the passion and talent of our great people can breathe fully.

When you introduce mastery, autonomy, and purpose into the office, you're driving something that's much more important than motivation. You're driving inspiration. While we can't truly motivate someone, we can inspire them. The difference is both subtle and dramatic.

Imagine you're sitting in a comfy chair, and I decide I want you to get up and go to the wall across the room. How can I accomplish this? First, I could try to move you. That is, I could physically pull you out of your seat and drag you all the way to the wall. I would be doing all the work. No fun.

Second, I could try to motivate you, either through positive or negative reinforcement. With negative reinforcement, I'd use fear,

Special Teams

One of the best ways to increase mastery, autonomy, and purpose — while at the same time fixing the pipes of your agency — is through project teams. Empower a small group of people (autonomy) with the challenge to fix a broken system (mastery) in order to help the organization and the people it serves (purpose).

When they're done right (which I'll talk about in Chapter 11), these projects are like booster shots of the flow state. Think of the scene in *Apollo 13* when the engineers, armed with nothing more than a box, duct tape, a tube sock, and a few spare parts, had to create an air filter to save the crew's life. Our projects in government don't usually involve life-and-death decisions, but done right, our people can be equally as engaged, successful, and satisfied as those men were.

threats, and consequences to get you out of the chair. If the consequences were severe enough, you would move. But you'd only move just enough to avoid the consequence. I'd have to threaten you all the way to the wall. Again, who is motivated here? I'd still be doing the work — I'd be pushing you. With positive reinforcement, I would use praise, reward, and recognition to get you out of the chair. If the reward were good enough, you would move, but, again, only enough to get the reward. To move you further I'd have to praise or reward you again. Most people think positive reinforcement is more effective. Well, it is more humane, but it's not more effective. I'm still the one who is motivated. I'm not pushing you to the wall, but instead I'm pulling you to it. Motivation is energy to move. The energy is still all mine.

So how do I get you to the wall using your energy, not mine? Inspiration. That is, I need to paint such a compelling picture of what is on that wall that you rise up out of the chair and run there yourself. I don't have to push, pull, or drag you. You are inspired by the future and move there of your own accord.

Inspiration creates an aim for others' intrinsic motivation. When we try to motivate, we expend the energy and we have to do it for each employee. But when we inspire, we spend the energy once — we paint the great picture and leave it up for all to see — and everyone who comes in contact with it is moved.

Attacking the Mold at its Source

Inspiring people to love their work is important, but it still leaves us with some moldy thinking: As long as you're locked into the notion that the people are the problem, you're never going to improve government. As we learned in the previous chapter, you can't motivate people or hold them accountable, and you're not going to get any new ones. So what can you do to create the mold-free, actively engaged workplace we're all seeking?

1. Stop it. All that other stuff — the mold creators — just knock it off. Tear down the posters, stop moving people's cheese, cancel the performance reviews. Just stop it. If you do nothing else, just stopping will make it better. It may not eradicate the mold, but at least it will stop adding to it. As British management guru John Seddon says, "Doing less of the wrong thing is not doing the right thing." Just stop.

2. Change the lens by which you view people. We are not children. We are not pets. We are not whales, mice, or penguins. (So put away your "Whale Done!", "Fish!", and other employee motivation strategies.) We are complex beings with complex needs and motivations. What gets a rat to push a button does not necessarily help a division manager overcome an egotistical boss, or a mental health case worker complete a complex multidisciplinary diagnosis. Just because a whale does a flip when you pat its nose doesn't mean the two rival units are going to like your reorganization plan. We need to see and treat each other as adult human beings.

That's Un-American!

Cancel performance reviews? We have to do them! It's the law!

One of my all-time favorite books is *Abolishing Performance Appraisals,* by Tom Coens and Mary Jenkins. After reading their masterful point-by-point tear-down of the supposed validity of performance reviews, there's simply no way to support these mold-creating instruments of torture. You've got to read it for yourself, but here's the main thesis: Performance reviews do more harm than good.

So why do we keep doing them? Well, for now, we're legally required to. And until enough people get enlightened on the accountability trap, the difference between systems and people, and the distinction between motivation and inspiration, we're stuck with performance reviews.

How can you meet that legal mandate without spreading mold?

Early in my career I facilitated a project to revamp an agency's performance appraisals. They had been a major sore spot for both managers and employees. Employees thought they were biased and unfair. Managers, seeking to avoid conflict, wouldn't do them, and HR was upset that the reviews weren't being completed annually. We conducted extensive focus groups with management and staff. Everyone screamed the exact same thing: "Why in the heck are we doing these?"

Management author Peter Scholtes laments that most of our organizational cultures, rather than being populated by adult-to-adult relationships, instead are dominated by parent-child relationships. When we see others as children, we treat them accordingly. We try to direct them and control them. We punish them and praise them.

The team came up with a bold solution: Let's just stop. Nobody likes them, they create conflict, and we gain nothing by doing them. Instead, the team came up with a perfectly logical replacement: a pass/fail system. Either your performance was fine and nothing happened to you, or you weren't fine and you began a journey of progressive discipline, shepherded by the good people of HR. No five-point scale, no 360-degree review, no rankings. Adults treating each other like adults.

Unfortunately, that's where the logic broke down. An infantile senior manager in the team presentation was outraged to hear he'd no longer be assigning letter grades or rankings. "What you are recommending is completely un-American!" he shouted. "Our country was founded on individual excellence. What did they give you in kindergarten? A grade. And first, and second grade? A grade. Pass/fail is un-American!"

Now, I've been called a lot of things in my career. But I've never had my patriotism questioned over an improvement project. Of course, the manager was inadvertently proving our point. Grades perpetuate a kindergarten culture. If you want the dynamic in your workplace to be one of teacher-versus-misbehaving-student, then by all means keep up those performance reviews.

If they please us, they get a reward. If they displease us, they get a talking-to. With this mentality, all organizational progress takes the same energy as getting a three-year-old to put his shoes on. All of the moldy things I described in the previous chapter create and perpetuate the parent-child relationship. The performance reviews, incentives, accountability talks, and goals. The training, behavioral changes, throwing fish, and reward programs. All of it ends when we change the lens — when we see everyone around us as the talented, contributing adults that they are.

Could you imagine sitting around at one of your volunteer service groups and telling everyone that they should all do 360-degree reviews of each other? Could you imagine hanging a Successories poster up in the dugout of your softball team? In almost every area of our life, we work together, shoulder-to-shoulder, equal with other adults. At PTA meetings, church fundraisers, and Little League games, there's no motivational artifice, no need to hold each other accountable. If your workplace culture is rampant with a parent-child mentality (even if it's a really-progressive-yoga-organic-mommy with empowered-self-expressing-young-adult), take stock and look for the source. Are there certain individuals who act like children? Send them to a different play pen. Does the boss really like being the parent?

One piece of child-rearing wisdom that does apply to the workforce is the idea that people tend to live up to the expectations that we have of them. If you tell a child that she's hopeless or nothing but trouble, she will prove you right. Tell that same child that she's amazing and smart and talented, and she will prove you right again. It's not just changing your words. It's changing the lens through which you see people. Some people make it hard to do, but everyone has good in them. Everyone has gifts. Rather than looking at your employees or co-workers and seeing only their flaws, learn to look past those flaws and see them for who they really are. We are all flawed, insecure,

Voluntary Effort

One of the best pieces of advice I received in my career was to treat my employees as if they were volunteers. Sure, they aren't. I pay them and we have contractual obligations. But "I pay them" is not enough motivation. Pay gets the ordinary effort. But what of the discretionary effort? The voluntary effort? How do you capture that? You have to recruit it. How do you get volunteers? You recruit them by giving them a compelling reason to get involved — mastery, autonomy, and purpose. How do you keep them? You have to keep recruiting them. You have to keep giving them interesting things to do, new skills to grow, and a strong sense of purpose.

Typically, we figure that once we've hired someone, the recruiting is over. It's like many men's view of marriage: "I told you I loved you at the wedding; if anything changes I'll let you know." Unfortunately, you may find out the hard way that employees, like spouses, are looking for that love all the time.

selfish, and angry. We are also beautiful, compassionate, caring, and gentle. We are all of these things. We are human.

As public servants, we are often slow, cumbersome, and inflexible. But we are good. Our policies are indecipherable and unreasonable. But we are good. We don't answer the phone, and you can't find the info you need on the Web. But we are good. We are closed on weekends, major holidays, and even some holidays we made up for ourselves. But we are good. We cost a lot and spend even more. But we are good. We are men and women working on behalf of the citizens of this country to do the noble work our democracy deems essential. We are protecting children, saving lives, safeguarding bridges, rehabilitating inmates, preserving forest land, and promoting peace. We are processing travel vouchers, fixing computers, creating project plans, and accounting for the money that makes all these things happen.

When we can learn to embrace all the good in ourselves, we can accept all of it in those around us. Our thoughts create our reality. When we focus on the negativity and the dysfunction, we tend to get more of it. When we go through life complaining, life tends to give us more things to complain about. When we see the good in everyone, there is more good to see. When we practice gratitude, it's amazing how life gives us more things to be grateful for. As the motivational author Wayne Dyer says, "When we change the way we look at things, the things we look at change."

3. Apply holistic medicine. For decades, we've tried treating the symptoms of mold — the lethargy, the in-fighting, the poor customer service, the quality problems, and so on. And unfortunately the cures — outsourcing, changing personalities, "motivating" people, and holding them accountable — have only made the patient sicker. My good friend and colleague Blake Shaw describes the problem in government as a holistic one. We've been trying to heal the body, when the true cause of the illness is the mind and the spirit. Further, the medicine we have dispensed has devastating side effects, and the patients have become immune to it anyway. To truly transform government, we must change hearts and minds.

Changing our minds. As Tom Peters said, all significant change begins with mindset. What stands between the government we have and the one we want is right between our ears. We have amazingly limiting beliefs about who we are and what we can do. We believe:

- *That we are different.* That we don't make widgets, that we don't have customers or a bottom line. That the techniques that work in other industries can't possibly work here. The truth is that we are not different. All organizations are collections of systems designed to achieve a purpose. All work is a system. Private-sector systems exist to make money; ours exist to make a difference. But the systems function the same way.

- *That we are dysfunctional.* That the problems we face — high cost, poor customer service, lack of speed and responsiveness — are unique to government. That all the slow, inefficient, customer-hating people in the world gravitated to one industry. The truth is that we are not alone. The dysfunction is not in our genetic code. Rather, it is the inevitable consequence of any organization that doesn't make tangible widgets, has hostages for customers, and has multiple customers with competing interests. Whether it's private or public is irrelevant. Any organization with those factors struggles to improve.

- *That we have a people problem.* That the problems we face are due to our employees. That our people are unmotivated, unaccountable, and can't be trusted. That the way to get things done is hold people accountable for meeting measurable goals with stretch targets. The truth is that we have great people. Amazing people. These public servants are just stuck in bad pipes and broken systems, trying to do the best job they can. We don't need to motivate them, change them, or hold them accountable. We need to inspire them and then unleash their intrinsic motivation and their desire to make a difference. If you want to get more work out of people, help your people get more out of work.

Changing our hearts. It's hard to give someone a heart transplant, especially an involuntary one. But eventually it happens to all of us. Your heart changes the minute you realize life is not about you. For some, this happens the moment they hold their child for the first time. For others, it occurs when their ego overdoses on self-centeredness and they find themselves surrounded by shiny toys and nobody to share them with. It happens to everyone eventually. In an epiphany, the secret is whispered into your subconscious ear: The more you help others, the more you help yourself. The moment you realize that life is about serving others is the moment you get everything you want in life, while simultaneously realizing that the only thing you want is to serve others.

We live to serve and we should do it spectacularly. No matter what you think your job is, according to spiritual author Marianne Williamson, your real job is to increase love in the world. Every job exists

What About the Really Bad Apples?

I know, I know. Despite everything I'm telling you, I haven't met Marge from Accounts Payable. She's awful. She's bitter, angry, uncooperative. She does half the work of any other employee and complains that she's overworked. Well, I *do* know Marge. I run into her everywhere I go. We all have a Marge. Roughly 6 percent of our workforce is Marge-like. So what should we do about it?

1. Don't drag the other 94 percent down. Typically, we try to fix Marge by creating policies, procedures, and consequences that apply to all the employees. We make the good performers jump through hoops and inhale mold because of Marge. Don't do that. Deal with Marge. If she is not producing to her capacity, talk to her about it. Don't create office-wide standards. She still won't meet them and everyone else's performance will drop to these minimum standards. If she comes to work wearing a halter top and a thong, talk to her about it. Don't create a forty-page dress code policy. The people we create the policies for won't follow them anyway. The people who follow them were the ones that didn't need them in the first place. Deal with problem individuals individually.

to serve someone. Every task is a chance to demonstrate the truth of who you really are — to demonstrate love.

There are few things more enjoyable than seeing someone who truly loves his work. Whether he's a teacher, an athlete, or a janitor, he does his job with youthful enthusiasm and he does it well. It becomes an exercise of joyful excellence.

2. Find out what her problem is. Was she like that when you hired her? If so, shame on you. If not, what happened? Is it a training issue or a desire issue? Does she have the skills to do the job as well as the information she needs?

3. Is this the right place for her? Each of us at some point in our careers has realized we were in the wrong spot. We weren't bad people; we just had a mismatch between our skills, our interests, and our assignment. Most of us, upon that realization, go find something else to do. Some people are not so quick to act and instead take their anxiety or boredom out in different, more destructive ways. Often, all we need to do is find a better fit for them. I can't tell you how many times I've seen a supposed bad apple turn into a delicious apple pie upon being reassigned.

4. If all the above options have been exhausted, it's time to free up Marge's future. It is an absolute imperative, provided you've tried all the above, that you help her move on. Poor performers are like tumors. Their apathy spreads quickly and drags down the health of everyone else. One of the biggest myths in government is that you can't fire anyone. You can. And, sometimes, you should.

What About the Really Good Apples?

You can do whatever you want for great performers — pat them on the back, recognize them, throw them a bonus. All of it will be appreciated. None of it will be required. They are great performers because they want to be. There's nothing wrong with recognizing their good work; just make sure you're clear about why you are doing it. If you are genuinely grateful for their contribution, then let them know. If you're doing it in hopes that it will motivate them or motivate others, save your breath. Instead, find ways to put them in flow-state situations. Give them new challenges, let them attend a class, have them speak to others about their successes. Simultaneously, get all the unnecessary, time-wasting stuff off their plates. Chances are, they're overloaded. Exempt them from staff meetings or pull them off the tech project that's dragging on forever. Make them go home or take a day off. Let them recharge and then give them something exciting to direct all their new energy toward.

I encountered this once in the most unlikely of places: a fast food restaurant at an airport in Atlanta. Fast-food restaurants typically aren't hot-beds of joy and excellence, and the airport ones are usually the worst. But as I waited in line, I couldn't help but notice the manager. She was moving at lightning speed, helping everyone in sight. Every two minutes she would sweetly shout to her employees, "Smile, ladies! Let them see your teeth!" She sent one of the workers out to the line to take our orders before we got to the counter. She then proceeded to walk throughout the food court asking each table how they liked their food and if she could bring them anything. In short, she acted like this was her restaurant. She cared about the customers, the employees, and the quality as if she had created the restaurant herself. She hadn't. She was a shift supervisor for a massive corporate fast-food conglomerate.

I couldn't take it anymore. After I finished my spicy chicken sandwich, I just had to ask her, "Why do you care so much? Why are you trying so hard?"

She was totally puzzled by my question, so I asked it in a different way. "You seem to be trying really hard. You care. Most people who do what you do don't care. They barely make eye-contact, much less come out to the seats to see if we like our food. Is it a customer-service contest you're in, or some profit-sharing thing for you?"

She was still puzzled. "No," she told me. "I get paid the same whether you like your sandwich or not."

"Then why do you care? Why do you do it?" (I couldn't believe how jaded that sounded coming out of my mouth.)

The expression on her face changed from bewilderment to the most beautiful compassion I'd seen this side of my wife or the Dalai Lama. She put her hand on my shoulder, stared warmly into my eyes, and said, "I do it for you."

Sometimes your worldview changes in an instant. This was one of those times. Serving people is our life's work. Excellence is its own reward.

CHAPTER 5

The Fable of Complexity

So just how do our pipes get so twisted, kinked, and gummed-up?
How does work get so complex and take so long? Read the following
fable and answer the questions at the end.

In the beginning, there was an important job to do. And Abby was the one to do it. Abby's job was to approve applications. For each applicant she:

- opened the submission (five seconds)
- reviewed the application for completeness (five minutes)
- analyzed the application (twenty minutes)
- approved or rejected the request (one minute)
- entered her decision and relevant information into the database (four minutes)

The total effort took about thirty minutes per application — some took more time, some took less. Customers got the response **the next day.**

And so it was, until …

One day, more applications came in than Abby could process in a day. She quickly got behind, and her customers let her know it. Stressed by the growing pile, the constant calls demanding status updates, and the feeling that she couldn't do a good job, Abby put in a request to management: "I need help!"

Management came to the rescue. Rather than give her help, they gave her a consultant. The consultant analyzed Abby's workload and quickly came to the conclusion that no one person could handle all that she did. Abby was relieved. She would soon have a co-worker who could take half the pile!

And so it was, until ...

The consultant report called for a major reorganization of Abby's job. No one person could do all the work Abby was doing. So the report recommended a solution:

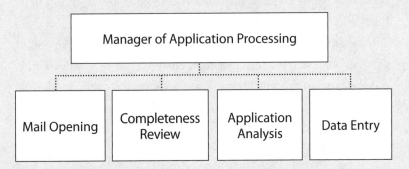

Each key task was assigned to specialists, with the ultimate approval of the application made by the manager, Elle. Abby would continue to analyze applications. Ben took care of opening the submissions. Carol reviewed the apps for completeness, and Dave handled data entry. After much change management training and many team-building exercises, they were ready for the ever-rising flow of applications into their office. Depending on Elle's availability, customers got a response within **three days.**

And so it was, until ...

One day, something came up missing. Carol blamed Ben's group, which had now grown to several people. Ben blamed Abby's group, which had also expanded quite a bit. Dave was just happy no one was yelling at his unit for a change. He'd learned a long time ago that the key to survival was to keep your head down. Elle ended the argument. "I don't care who lost it," said. "Just find it, and *never let it happen again!*"

Ben quickly went back to his work group and issued a new procedure. He said, "Look guys, Carol can no longer be trusted. From now on, before you give anything to Carol's reviewers, I want you to stack them in a pile of 100. On top of that pile, attach a cover sheet with your initials verifying that all 100 are accounted for."

Meanwhile, Carol, Abby and Dave implemented similar procedures, each ensuring that if something was missing, it wasn't their fault. Each application now waited until there was a pile of 100 at each station before moving on. Customers received their responses within **two weeks.**

And so it was, until …

One day, a very important customer, Mr. Smith, called. He was quite accustomed to prompt responses, but he'd been waiting on his current application for some time now. Elle promised to get to the bottom of the delay. She convened Abby, Ben, Carol, and Dave to the conference room and asked about the whereabouts of Mr. Smith's application.

Carol piped up first. "We can't possibly know where one application is. Each application is in a group of 100, and we have dozens of those groups running through our unit at a given time." Each of the others in the room nodded in agreement. They had similar procedures and the same problem.

Elle replied, "I can't tell Mr. Smith I don't know where his application is. Track it down, and *never let it happen again!*"

Ben quickly went back to his workgroup and issued a new procedure. He said, "Look guys, Elle is getting calls from customers wanting to know their status. We need to be able to answer those questions quickly and expedite the very important customers. From now on, we need to attach a tracking number to each application and enter that number in the TPS report. When we pass the pile to Carol's unit, change the status of all tracking numbers to indicate they are in Carol's unit, not ours."

Carol, Abby, and Dave implemented similar procedures allowing them to track the document and indicate whether it had left their work unit. A report was sent to Elle each week showing the applications received, their number and their status. When Elle received a call, she checked the report and could provide a quick answer to the caller and a quick nudge to the appropriate work unit to hurry up. Each application took a little longer to process, as numbers now had to be assigned, logged, and tracked. Most customers got their responses in **three weeks** — unless they called, in which case they would get it the next day.

And so it was, until …

One day, Elle got tired of answering phone calls. It seemed that she spent more time tracking down applications and expediting them than she did managing the work area. Elle put in a request to management: "I need help!"

Management came to the rescue. Rather than give her help, they gave her a consultant. The consultant analyzed her work and quickly came to the conclusion that she was spending too much time answering calls and not enough time managing. She spent five minutes on each call and almost 40 percent of customers were calling. The consultant recommended a phone center dedicated to answering calls and giving great customer service. Elle was relieved. She would soon have a customer service unit handling the ever-rising flood of phone calls!

And so it was, until …

Management approved the plan but not the budget. There simply wasn't any money available for adding new people. They recommended instead that Elle take resources from each of the work units to meet this very pressing need.

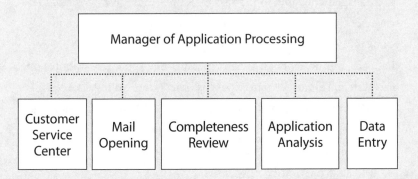

Each work unit coughed up a person and the new Customer Service Center was created. After much change management training and many team-building exercises, they were ready for the ever-rising flow of calls into their office. Each work unit now had fewer people to process applications, so customers got their responses within **six weeks.** (They got their calls answered quite promptly, though.)

And so it was, until …

One day, more calls came in than the Customer Service Center could handle. It seemed that the number of calls was growing exponentially every day, and the customers were growing more and more irate. Stressed by the abuse her employees were taking and by the constant turnover of her staff, Fran, the customer service supervisor, put in a request to management: "I need help!"

Management came to the rescue. Rather than give her help, they gave her a consultant. The consultant analyzed the call-center work and quickly came to the conclusion that they couldn't possibly keep up with all the calls that were coming in. Fran was relieved. She would soon have more customer service representatives to handle the ever-growing volume of calls!

And so it was, until ...

The consultant's report, in exchange for giving her more people from Abby, Ben, Carol, and Dave's units, demanded accountability from the customer service representatives. Using lots of statistics, the consultant determined that each phone rep should be able to answer ten calls per hour. Each call should take exactly five minutes, leaving ten minutes per hour for doing paperwork and restroom breaks. (Restroom time should be monitored to ensure that no one took too long.) Further, customer service reps who answered more than ten calls per hour were to be rewarded; those who took fewer than ten calls were to be punished.

Magically, all the calls got answered. Additionally, each rep was answering exactly eleven calls per hour. Each work unit now had fewer people to process applications, so customers got their responses within **eight weeks.**

And so it was, until ...

One day, Mr. Smith called Elle's boss, Gary. Mr. Smith was still a very important customer, and he demanded to know why things were now taking eight weeks. He had called the customer service number five times but was hung up on each time before getting his status question answered. He threatened to take this matter to the highest authority! Gary, faced with the long processing times and scared of what might happen if Mr. Smith got hold of the right people, put in a request to management: "I need help!"

Management came to the rescue. Rather than give him help, they gave him a consultant. The consultant analyzed the unit and quickly came to the conclusion that applications took too long to process. Gary was relieved that he would have more processors available to handle the flood of work coming into the organization.

And so it was, until ...

The consultant's report called for a timeliness standard. Using lots of statistics, the consultant demonstrated that applications took an average of eight weeks to process, but some took sixteen weeks. Everyone agreed these exceptions were unacceptable. They also agreed to a new standard that no application would take longer than twelve weeks to process. A new procedure was created that alerted Elle when an application was in Week 11. These applications were then given top priority. Flagging, prioritizing, and reassigning the work added about five minutes per application. All applications now took exactly **twelve weeks** to process.

And so it was, until …

One day, the organization faced a budget crisis. The cost to perform their vital function was outpacing the revenue. Stressed by what this might do to morale, the employees' careers, and their desire to make a difference, the senior management team declared: "We need help!"

They called a consultant. The consultant analyzed all the different divisions, sections, and functions and quickly came to the conclusion that the organization could no longer afford to do what it was doing. The management team was relieved. They would soon have increased capacity to do more good!

And so it was, until ...

The consultant's report recommended a reorganization — a cost-saving consolidation of all like functions across the organization. Rather than each unit having mail openers, there would be a central mail-processing facility. Likewise for data entry, call centers, and administrative functions. The design was modeled on Elle's work unit.

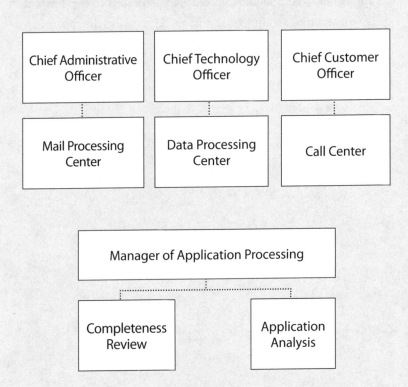

Each application would now be received in the Mail Processing Center, where it would be logged, opened, and sorted with all the other mail in the organization. Applications would be delivered to the Completeness Review Section every two days, unless another job was more pressing. After Elle had approved applications from Abby's analysis unit, a report was generated specifying how many applications needed to be data-processed. This report was used by the Chief Technology Officer to schedule data-entry resources and allocate costs back to Elle's unit. Most data-entry jobs were returned within two weeks. Calls regarding application status were handled by the central call center, which was building an electronic tracking system that each unit would soon comply with. After much change management training and many team building exercises, the organization was ready for the financial crisis. Elle's unit lost 50 percent of its staff to the reorganization. Customers got their responses within **six months.**

And so it was, until …

One day, the top boss, Mrs. Hill, went to a conference on best practices. She was wowed by PowerPoints from technology vendors showing how much money she could save if she automated her operations. After two bottles of wine at a fancy restaurant — and encouraged by the prospect of meeting her mandates at lower cost and with up-to-date technology — she said to the vendors: "I need help!"

The vendors came to the rescue. They glanced at the work processes, starting with Elle's unit, and quickly came to the conclusion that the agency's way of doing business was out of date. Mrs. Hill was relieved. She would soon have a modern, paperless system that would make her organization the best in its class!

And so it was until …

The vendors brought in shiny boxes and lots of coders and integrators. Rather than working with paper, new electronic procedures were established:

- The Mail Processing Center, at the end of each day, would send its work to the Chief Technology Officer to be assigned to a new scanning and imaging section. Each applicant would be imaged into the new system and assigned an electronic tracking number.

- An electronic report would be sent to Carol's unit to alert her to do a completeness review. Carol's unit would look at the document image to determine if the application was complete. Half the documents had a supporting attachment that couldn't be imaged with the main file and required a special request for the paper documents. These documents were delivered by the new Archive Retrieval Unit within two weeks.

- Upon completion of their review, Carol's unit logged into the new tracking system to change the document status update. Elle electronically approved the status changes weekly and, using the new workflow software, she could log on and pass the workflow to Abby's unit.

- An electronic record was sent to Abby's unit alerting them to begin processing the next batch of applications. Working from the imaged documents, they were required to enter their comments and notes in the new Application Review Database. Each application was given a code number, which was matched with each reviewer number, allowing anyone to easily see which application was assigned to which worker and what comments they made.

- Upon completion of the review, an electronic report was sent to Elle to complete the approvals. She had to log on to the system by each reviewer number and electronically sign off on their recommendations. She then logged into the tracking system to signify that their work unit was finished with the file.

- An electronic report was sent to the central data-entry unit to complete the record in the Application Database and print the response letters. The response letters were logged in the tracking system and an electronic request was sent to the Mail Processing Center to send the letters. That request was used by the Chief Administrative Officer to assign work and allocate costs back to the Chief Technology Officer. Approval letters were mailed out by the central mail facility every Friday, unless there was a more pressing job in the queue.

After $120 million, six years, much change management training and many team-building exercises, they were ready to meet the ever-rising flow of applications into the office. Customers got their initial response in **fifty-three weeks** — one week after they were supposed to begin the annual renewal process.

Key questions

1. To what do you attribute the complexity that this process took on?

2. By the end, how long did it take a customer to get approval?

3. How much work time — actual labor — goes into processing an approval?

4. Where does the water get stuck in the pipe?

5. What would you have done with Abby's original request for more people?

6. What would you have done with Elle's request for phone help?

7. What role did technology play in improving this process?

8. How engaged do you think this workforce is?

9. Draw the pipe using the diagram on the next page.

10. Now redesign the pipe however you wish. How long would it take customers to receive their approval? How many employees would you need? Assume each application takes thirty minutes of work and the organization receives 100 applications a day.

5 Essential Questions

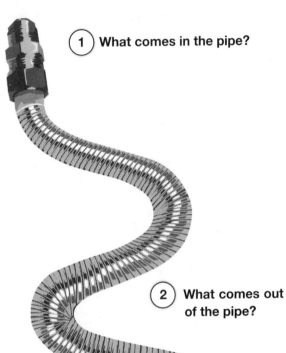

1. What comes in the pipe?

2. What comes out of the pipe?

3. Who uses it?

4. Why?

5. How long does it take them to get it?

The Moral of the Story

Ah, sweet complexity. And it all comes from one place: CYA.

CYA is the fundamental building block of complexity. If you take any complex process and stick it under a microscope to examine its DNA, you will find one common thing: CYA. Something goes wrong, somebody gets kicked, and they build up defenses.

So why do we have so much CYA? The obvious answer is that, well, we're government. We work in a fishbowl. Anytime something goes wrong in government, it ends up in the news. Not only can we *not* sweep it under a rug, we *have* to share it with the whole world in public hearings, public information requests, and newspaper headlines. There's nothing we can do about that.

But there's another reason we have so much CYA, and it's one we can do something about: handoffs. Just as we saw in the fable, every time you have a handoff, you eventually end up with CYA. It doesn't start that way. Most processes begin with little complexity. Person A does all the work. But over time, the pressures on A become too much, and we add B. But rather than having B do the same work A was doing, we give part of it to A part of it to B. Now we have a handoff. And eventually we add C and D and E and F.

These handoffs create their own problems, which we will discuss in a moment. But the main problem is that handoffs cause CYA. Eventually, life happens. Something goes wrong. Person A gives something to Person B, who claims she never got it. Or D can't find something and blames it on C or B. And just as in the fable, the big boss comes along and says, "Find it and *never let it happen again*."

That one phrase is the source of all complexity in our organizations.

You get blamed for something, and it's human nature that you don't want to get blamed again. So you build up defense mechanisms — tracking sheets, logging systems, and so on. The goal shifts from getting the work done to not getting blamed for when the work does not get done. The root cause of complexity is CYA. The root cause of CYA is handoffs. Which begs the question: Why do we have so many handoffs?

The reason we have so many handoffs is because Adam Smith was a pinhead.

You may remember Adam Smith from high school economics. Adam Smith was the grandfather of modern economic theory. In 1776, Adam Smith was studying pin-makers. These were skilled craftsmen in guilds making pins. Think about what the economy was like in 1776. You essentially had two types of workers. You had skilled craftsmen organized in guilds and you had farmers. Okay, there were some lawyers and doctors around, too. But for the most part, you were either a craftsman or a farmer. Now, if you wanted to buy a chair in 1776, you wouldn't hop in the buggy and head to Wal-Mart or Ikea. No, you'd go to a skilled craftsman in a guild, and he would build the entire chair from beginning to end. And so it was with the pin-makers that Adam Smith was studying. These craftsmen would build sewing pins from beginning to end.

But in 1776 the economy was going through a major change. This was the cusp of the Industrial Revolution. The demand for goods from customers was beginning to outstrip what skilled craftsmen could provide. The craftsman simply did not have the capacity to meet the demand. Sound familiar?

In order to meet this growing demand, people moved from the farms to the city to help with production.

That created two problems. First, the farmers moving to the cities were not skilled craftsmen. They were largely unskilled and uneducated, and there wasn't a whole lot of technology to support them. Second, there wasn't enough time for these individuals to become skilled craftsmen. Those craftsmen had learned their trade over many years serving as apprentices and journeymen. Now, a whole new workforce was being rushed in, and they did not have the same skills.

In order to meet the demand and accommodate the low-skilled, uneducated workforce, jobs that had been handled from beginning to end now got broken up and specialized. So, for the pin-makers, Smith wrote: "One man draws out the wire, another straightens it, a third cuts it, a fourth points it, a fifth grinds it at the top for receiving the head. ..."

Smith's observations begat Division of Labor, which led to the assembly line, which created our general approach to how we make widgets in this world.

For many of us, that way of thinking still pervades our cubicles. What used to be a generalist task has now been split up across ten to twelve different handoffs in three different sections. This kind of specialization made sense in the context of 1776. But is that the way our workforce looks today? Are government workers unskilled and uneducated? Do we have crude technology? I would argue it's the exact opposite.

When you're dealing with unskilled, uneducated workers, the key is simplicity. Design a job that's so simple, nobody could mess it up. But in order to accommodate *task simplicity,* we in turn create *process complexity.* When we chop up work into that many small, simple pieces, the process then involves a lot of coordination and a lot of handoffs and a lot of management.

There's a newer way of thinking about work that's been evolving over the past thirty years. It turns the Division of Labor equation on its head, by focusing on *task complexity* and *process simplicity.* Our workers today are smarter, higher-skilled and have greater access to technology. In turn, they can do more. They can take on a greater variety of tasks, with more complexity and, often, at a higher volume. Meanwhile, our processes become very simple, because there's no need for all the handoffs that accommodate specialization. A process

All the King's Horses

"... [I]t is a consequence of what we call the Humpty Dumpty School of organizational management. Companies take a natural process, such as order fulfillment, and break it into lots of little pieces — the individual tasks that people in the functional departments do. Then, the company has to hire all the king's horses and all the king's men to paste the fragmented work back together again. These king's horses and king's men have titles such as auditor, expediter, controller, liaison, supervisor, manager, and vice president. They are simply the glue that holds together the people who do the real work — the credit checkers, the inventory pickers, the package shippers. In many companies, direct labor costs may be down, but overhead costs are up — way up. Most companies today, in other words, are paying more for the glue than for the real work — a recipe for trouble."

— from *Reengineering the Corporation,*
by Michael Hammer and James Champy

with two handoffs is fundamentally simpler to manage and less costly than a process with twelve handoffs. Under the old way of thinking, our pipes get long and twisted and convoluted. Under the new way, our pipes are short, straight, and simple.

And that's the real driver of complexity: How do you see your people? Do you view them the old way or the new way? Do you see them as unskilled, uneducated, and unworthy of your trust? Or do you see them as knowledgeable, skillful, and trustworthy?

How you answer that question will make all the difference in the way that your organization gets work done. The key ingredient is trust.

This is exactly what I was talking about in the chapter about mold. The mold is our view of people. If we view them as lazy, incompetent, and untrustworthy, our organization will reflect that. The mold that we see creeping throughout the hallways in government, fouling the air and making us sick, is the rampant distrust of our employees.

What is trust? It's a word we throw around like "beauty" or "justice." Can we actually do anything about it? Is it manageable? Trust is made up of two components. In order for me to trust you, I have to believe, first, that you're competent to do the job I'm asking you to do, that you have the skills and the ability to pull it off. The second component of trust is caring. Do I believe that you care about me? You may have all the skills in the world, but you may honestly not care whether or not the job gets done. Trust is made up of both components.

For example, I have a real trust issue with my family when it comes to getting to church on Sunday morning. On the one hand, we have my son. For whatever reason, on a Sunday morning, my son is never able to locate and put on his shoes. Any other day of the week, if a friend knocks at the door or my son wants to play basketball, his shoes are on his feet in five seconds or less. But trying to get out the door on Sunday morning? Forty-five minutes for him to find his shoes. Is that an issue of competence or caring? Clearly, it's a caring issue. The boy knows how to put on shoes; he just doesn't want to on Sunday.

On the other hand, we have my wife. My wife very much wants to go to church. Yet we still have to move heaven and earth to get in the car and make it to the church, and even then we're usually fifteen minutes late. For my wife, it's not an issue of caring. She wants to be there. It's a competence issue. My wife (who I am completely enamored with and continually in awe of all that she does) was unfortunately born without that part of the human genome that can tell time and divide up the day accordingly. She always tries to pack twenty things into a unit of time that will only accommodate two.

In both cases, either my son's inability to find and put on shoes or my wife's inability to manage the clock, I end up having to manage the whole process. And the process becomes rife with CYA. We get up earlier and earlier each week. I have to give detailed instructions and inspect, monitor, and incentivize each week. We have to check and recheck how many heads are in the car. We batch children together so we don't lose any. We craft new policies and communicate them. We institute new training and team building. It's an enormous amount of effort, and all for one reason: lack of trust.

Caring and competence. We can't do much about the first one (although we can try to make people care by inspiring them and appealing to their sense of purpose, as I discussed in the previous chapter). What we can do, and what we absolutely must do, is to help improve employees' competence. If a lack of trust in the workplace is based on the concern that workers don't have the right skills, it's the responsibility of managers to develop those skills.

Let's step back and put this in context. Developing individuals' skills and then putting them back into a broken system isn't going to help us out. We first have to improve the system, straighten the pipes, and remove as many of the system constraints to individual productivity as we can. But once we've done all those things to improve the system, then by all means we need to focus intently on developing the skills and capacity of the individuals.

I'm reminded of a manufacturing organization I met with several years ago. This was a world-class manufacturer, but they were confronted with escalating CYA costs. Their operations had grown more and more complex, and the senior managers were having trouble understanding how it had gotten it that way. As they were discussing all these issues, one manager wrote a question on a napkin and passed it around: "Do we trust our employees?" Their answer was unanimous.

They didn't. After much more soul-searching, they realized why. Their employees didn't have the skills they needed to do their jobs. These were blue-collar workers, and as the manufacturing tasks had grown more advanced, their skill set hadn't.

The company was faced with a dilemma: simplify the work (which would create even more complex processes and drive up costs) or build up the capabilities of the workforce. The organization committed 10 percent of its operating budget to employee development, working with each individual employee to determine areas for improvement, and the company funded their growth and development. As the employees' competence improved, so did the trust relationship — in both directions. With more trust came more responsibility. With more responsibility came greater task complexity. With greater task complexity came process simplicity.

The root cause of complexity is CYA. The root cause of CYA is handoffs. The root cause of handoffs is specialization. The root cause of specialization is distrust. All of the process-improvement tools in the world are of no use if we don't trust our workforce.

The Crazy Cycle

The second moral of the fable has to do with the "crazy cycle." It's a phenomenon that begins the moment we first get behind in our work. As soon as we get just a little bit behind, we're destined to get really far behind. We get backlogged. The secret to dealing with backlog is never to get behind in the first place — not even for a moment.

Here's how the crazy cycle works. Let's say we run an agency that grants environmental permits. Our customers get used to a certain turnaround time for getting their permits. Suddenly one day, we get a little behind. It's no big deal; we're just a little bit swamped. But what do our customers do? They call. They want to know where their permits are. So we take time to answer the calls, find out where their stuff is and let them know. That's time we can't spend actually processing the permits. And now, thanks to the time off we had to take to handle the phone calls, we're even further behind. That leads to more phone calls, more time spent answering them and more time spent tracking down permits. Which leads to even more delays. Before you know it, we're spending more time answering phone calls and tracking stuff down than we ever spent on the actual work itself.

Does this sound familiar? How do we stop the madness?

The knee-jerk fix for the crazy cycle is a technological one. If everyone's asking, "Where's my stuff?" we try to find a way to get that answer quickly. So we build an electronic tracking system to tell us where each customer is in the process. That's right, we divert even more precious resources — which could be used to *do* the work — to *track* the work. (I have seen no fewer than ten of these in the past month — each with a price tag over $20 million.) Insane.

Here's a dose of sanity: If your process is so messed up that you have to spend $20 million to tell you how far behind you are, then perhaps you are working on the wrong thing. You don't need the tracking system — you need to fix the process! Speed up the process and the phone calls will go down. Fewer phone calls means fewer resources devoted to answering them, which means more resources to do the work, which means less backlog, which means fewer calls. Now *that's* a cycle you want to be on.

CYA and the crazy cycle. Together they wreak havoc on our home — spreading mold and gumming up our pipes. Fortunately the solution to both problems is the same: We have to go faster. Way, way, way faster.

Turning Down Call Volume

Sometimes, getting off the crazy cycle works even better than anticipated. I once worked with a tax agency that had worked out a radical process redesign allowing them to deliver tax refunds 80 percent faster. Their plan was to reduce the number of calls from angry customers by completing the process so quickly that citizens never had a chance to call in the first place. If you got your refund before you ever had a chance to wonder where it was, you'd never call, and the agency could actually focus on its work.

But when we looked at the call statistics, we found the agency was getting as many calls as ever before. Astonished, we ran to the phone center and started listening to the calls. Turns out the citizens were still calling, but not to ask, "Where's my check?" Instead, they were asking, "What's this check I got in the mail? Is it okay if I cash it?"

Once citizens got used to getting their refunds quickly, the calls dropped precipitously.

CHAPTER 6

Faster

For years, I traveled across the country conducting workshops called "Better Faster Cheaper." Before each class, we'd conduct a pre-call with attendees to see what their specific objectives were. Nine times out of ten, they would say, "We're definitely interested in the better and the cheaper part, but the faster part really doesn't apply to us." Some would even ask if we could skip that part because it made their bosses nervous. Or sometimes the reaction to "fast government" was a bit more animated. I was introducing the topic to a group of regulatory commissioners and hadn't gotten ten minutes into it before one of them, red-faced and swollen, interrupted me, saying, "This is nonsense! A fast government is a totalitarian government! American government was designed by our founders to be slow."

Nice try. The *policy-making* of government — Should we go to war? What will our building codes be? Who will be taxed what amount? — was designed to be slow and deliberate, and I agree that it should be. But the operations of government are a totally different matter. Deploying forces to war, completing building inspections, issuing tax refunds — those are all meant to be speedy and efficient. Establishing the role of government should take some time. Executing that role should not.

Whatever the reason, we in government have a natural aversion to speed. But we need to get over it — quickly. Why? Well, for one thing, the world is speeding up. Thomas Friedman sold about a trillion books arguing that the world was flat. He left out a chapter. The world is also tilted — downhill. Everything in life is speeding up. Not only can we check our email, get directions to a restaurant, and read the reviews from past customers all on one portable device, we absolutely flip out if it takes more than a nanosecond to download any of it. A trip that took our forefathers several months in a covered wagon — battling tuberculosis and bears along the way — today takes us a three-hour plane ride. And we're apoplectic if the plane takes off half an hour late. Absent some *Mad Max*-style apocalyptic catastrophe or a rash of celebrities converting to the Amish way of life, I don't believe this ever-faster trajectory will change.

Another reason we need to overcome our fear of speed is that our customers demand it. Want a preview of what's going to happen to your agency over the next decade? Look no further than the DVR box sitting under your television. TiVo and other DVR systems have warped our concept of time. You can go forward in time, backward in time and even pause time (which I personally hate, because it has ruined my "I'll take out the trash after the game" excuse). DVRs have fundamentally disrupted the TV power structure. Before DVRs, the customer was hostage to the network. You watched what they wanted you to watch, when they wanted you to watch it, complete with unavoidable commercials. DVRs freed the hostages. When is your favorite show on? Whenever you want! You call the shots now. Like it or not, ours has become an on-demand world. Is your agency an on-demand operation?

And the same thing goes for your employees. The incoming generations of new workers have been raised with a push-button mentality. Movies, news, TV shows, songs — for them, it's all always been available at the touch of a button. They won't tolerate working in a slow environment — starting with the three- or four-month hiring process that's typical in government agencies. If you want to recruit those workers — and given the waves of Baby Boom retirees, you don't really have a choice — you're going to have to speed your hiring process. And once those employees are in the door, they simply won't accept the old, slow ways of getting things done.

Fast government: Our customers demand it, our employees demand it and, as you will soon see, it's the only way we will meet the great challenges our government is facing. Remember what I detailed in the beginning of this book? All of government's problems are one problem — capacity. Out-of-control budgets, customer dissatisfaction, employee disengagement, and long lines all exist primarily because there's more coming in than going out. We have too much water coming into our twisted, kinked-up, gummed-up pipes. And as I explained earlier, the only real way to fix this problem is to straighten the pipes. Speed the flow.

But won't greater speed lead to more mistakes? Won't quality suffer? No. And this is where it's important to explain what's actually going faster.

I worked with one organization for several years to help speed its operations. Before implementing any major change, we would convene a session to demonstrate the concepts. I keenly remember one of these sessions, because it was the first time I genuinely feared for my safety. The session was scheduled to start at 9 a.m., but at 8:55 the general counsel of the organization came storming in. This man was a big, tough, Harley Davidson-riding guy, and he lit into me before he even sat down.

"So you're the one, huh?" he yelled at me. "You're the one who's gonna make me work 80 percent faster."

"I don't think so," I replied, backpedaling into the wall.

"Well, that's what they told me!" he said. "I was told to come to this class and learn to work 80 percent faster." (His language, by the way, was much, much more colorful than I'm quoting here.) "What am I supposed to do? Read my law books faster? Type my opinions quicker? Talk faster?"

"I'm afraid you got the wrong idea, sir," I said, my voice cracking like Peter Brady's. "This class is about going 80 percent faster, but not about *you* going faster."

He seemed puzzled.

"Let me ask you this," I said. "You produce legal opinions. How long does it typically take for your customers, the requesting parties, to get a response?"

He hemmed and hawed and listed all the exceptions, but finally said it takes about three months. "Perfect," I said. "About three months. Now, all of the reading and typing and communicating you were describing before, how long does that take? That is, if you had everything you needed, and could just sit down uninterrupted and crank one out, how long would that take?"

He gave a profanity-laced explanation of how I didn't understand how the real world worked, and that he never had the resources he needed or the time to focus on getting one thing done. I told him I understood — and I reassured him that my head doesn't actually fit where he had suggested it did. I tried to pin him down again.

"The time to just do the work?"

"Just do the work," I said.

"About three hours," he finally offered.

"So it takes you three hours, but the customers wait three months?" I said, while ducking.

He went off again.

"The requestor never knows what they really want! We gotta read it five times and then send back a letter asking for clarification! Once we finally get them straight on what the hell *they* want, we gotta show it to a committee to get *their* opinion. Then we do a draft, and we gotta circulate it to a list of people as long as your arm. Each one of *those* little pissants puts their two cents in, and we gotta change it and send it to all of them again. *Then* they change their mind and switch it all back. And for some reason the director treats signing the thing like she's signing over one of her kidneys. You try running that maze in three hours!"

"All that stuff?" I said. "That's what this class is about."

He went on to become one of our fiercest advocates.

You see, when I talk about going faster, I'm not talking about making the tasks go faster. I'm talking about the space *between* the tasks. That's where the opportunity lies. It's not about reading faster or typing faster or skimming instead of studying. It's all the lost time between the reading, the typing, and the studying.

The actual work time — the labor in a process — typically consumes less than 5 percent of the total time a customer experiences. Ninety-five percent of the time a customer spends in our pipes,

Give It a Try Yourself

- Think about the key pipe for your agency or work unit — what comes out of the pipe?

- How long does it take a customer to get it?

- If you locked the key players in a room and didn't let them out until all the tasks were done, how long would that take?

- What is the percent difference?

- Where did all the time go?

nothing is happening. Does that mean we're sitting around doing nothing 95 percent of the time? Not at all. We are doing a million other things. But for that one customer, that one transaction, only 5 percent of the elapsed time has involved actual work time. We have a 95 percent opportunity, so we can at least grab 80 percent, right?

Two Concepts of Time

WORK TIME: The amount of time in a process where work (labor) is actually occurring.

ELAPSED TIME: The total amount of time a process takes, from the customers' perspective

Let's use an example from your workplace: your expense reimbursement. Say you go out of town on a business trip and you want to get reimbursed for your expenses. How long, from your perspective as the customer of the system, does it take to get reimbursed? The clock starts the moment the money leaves your pocket and ends the moment the money is back in your pocket. For most agencies, it takes about two to four weeks. Do you really think there is someone in payroll toiling over your reimbursement check for four straight weeks? No. There's about five minutes of hard labor for each check. Where did the rest of the time go? The system — the laws, rules, policies, and procedures, plus all the CYA. The handoffs, batching, backlog, bottlenecks, and technology glitches. The secret to paying you more quickly is not to stand over the payroll clerks yelling, "Mush!" It's figuring out where the four weeks went.

Okay, so you're on board with me. You're ready to increase capacity and speed the flow by straightening the pipes. But how exactly do we do that?

Get ready to roll up your sleeves. Here are five strategies to make

Why Only 80 Percent?

I talk a lot about making processes run 80 percent faster. But why not 95 percent, if that's the gap between elapsed time and actual work time? It comes down to the return on effort: Once you start digging in to this, you'll discover that going 80 percent faster is actually quite doable. Getting that last 15 percent? Not as easy. So grab the 80 percent. If you get more, great. Less? That's okay too. Eighty percent improvement would be stellar, but whether you improve your speed by 80 percent, 75 percent, 50 percent, or 20 percent, you're still vastly improving your agency's capacity.

your systems faster. They're focused on that 95 percent of the time that gets lost in the system — not the 5 percent in which the actual labor takes place. These strategies are counterintuitive and often fly in the face of what are usually considered best practices. (That's how I know they're good.) Not all five will be relevant to your own agency's pipes, but some will. As you read these, visualize your pipes and think about how you can start straightening them out.

Strategy #1: Triage

Most pipes in government are of the one-size-fits-all variety. We have one long, twisted pipe, and we make every customer travel through it. One of the most powerful strategies for speeding the flow is to actually create more pipes — that is, give customers other pathways they can travel.

Customers accessing our pipes tend to break into three large categories. On one end of the spectrum is the self-service customer. He knows your pipes better than you do and needs minimal assistance to get the job done. On the other end of the spectrum is the intensive-care client. He knows nothing and can do nothing, and therefore needs his hand held through every step of the process. In the middle are your moderates. They don't need as much assistance as the intensive-care clients but also aren't quite ready to fly solo. Each of these customer groups could use a different pipe. Unfortunately, we often send them all down the pipe together. We waste precious resources assisting self-help clients, which then robs us of capacity to provide intensive care. We need a different pipe for each type — and we need a good triage system for directing customers to the right one.

Let's think about this in terms of an agency that approves building permits. Developers seeking permits tend to fall into three categories: frequent flyers, who develop lots of properties in the county every year; once-in-a-lifetimers, such as the guy with some extra land who wants to develop it into a shopping mall; and those in between. The once-in-a-lifetime developers aren't at all familiar with the permitting process or the codes, and they won't understand anything your agency sends them. They need you to walk them through the entire process. The frequent flyers know the permit process better than the agency does. (In fact, they probably hired the best person from the agency to come lead their government affairs division.) These two customer groups require different pipes. The intensive-care pipe is obvious, but what would you do for frequent flyers? The innovation in many places has been to move from inspecting their plans to inspecting their process. That is, the agency certifies the people and the process used during development and then audits compliance with the process. Rather than inspecting the hundreds of building plans the frequent flyers submit, the agency instead inspects the pipes of the developer. What qualifications do their planners have? What process do they use to ensure quality in their plan development? How well do they train on building codes and enforcement standards?

Instant Coffee

Starbucks (where, incidentally, a large portion of this book was written) had a problem with the drive-thru lanes at its suburban stores. The lines of cars kept getting longer and longer, and the poor, uncaffeinated souls inside the cars kept waiting longer and longer to get their java fix. The company tried to address the lack of speed using a corporate-wide program to blame and retrain the baristas. Starbucks turned to a manufacturing technique called 5S. In a nutshell, 5S ensures that everything a worker needs to do her job is organized in such a way that she can reach it or utilize it with as little motion as possible. Starbucks hired manufacturing experts to work with baristas to redesign their workspaces, moving the whipped cream closer to the cinnamon, the blender closer to the ice, and so on.

But the line at the drive-thru still stretches around the block. Why? Because Starbucks worked on the wrong end of the problem. The new 5S approach helped trim some work time, but what about the elapsed time? The 95 percent?

Across town from Starbucks we have a Caribou Coffee. It's too far for me to drive each day, but when I do go, I marvel at Caribou's brilliantly simple solution to the same drive-thru dilemma. Caribou has two drive-thru lanes. One lane is only for coffee; the other is for all the goofy half-caf extra-whip soylent green macchiato drinks. Coffee takes twenty seconds to pour and I'm out of there. Starbucks leaves me in line behind these twenty-minute pieces of coffee art.

Both sides have a vested interest in making this radical approach work. By getting the hundreds of plans out of their shop while still ensuring quality work, the agency can spend more time with the novice and moderate developers. By meeting the certification standards and passing the audits of the agency, the developer gets to keep his plans out of the log jam and consequently can minimize development delays. Where these partnerships are working, the two sides have actually become allies to improve the ordinances, codes, and the internal development process for all developers. Putting intensive-care customers through a self-service pipe is ineffective and cruel. And putting self-service customers through an intensive-care model is expensive and cruel as well.

When I talk to government folks about this concept of triage and express lanes, I'm usually greeted with great skepticism. There simply is no way to make the pipe faster, they tell me. It takes six weeks, end of story. But then I ask how long it takes if the big boss or the top elected official calls. Oh, in that case, they say, we'll expedite it and get it out in a couple of days.

Exactly. The treatment for the Big Kahuna is possible for the everyday Joe. The expedited process is usually just the work time, with all of the elapsed time — the time lost in batches, backlogs, bottlenecks and CYA — stripped away. Your expedited process should be your everyday process — at least for most of your customers.

Strategy #2: Simultaneous Processing

One of the side effects of Adam Smith's Division of Labor and government's propensity for specialization is that we have built long, sequential processes. Our pipes are divided into sections, and the water must travel through these sections one at a time. For example, building permits move from plan reviewers to code enforcement to the fire marshal and then the public health department. Your expense account goes to your supervisor, then her boss, then his boss, and then over to accounting, where it is reviewed and then processed and then approved. One of the simplest tactics for moving water through our pipes more quickly is to use simultaneous or parallel processing.

To understand the principle of simultaneous processing, let's go back to *Extreme Makeover: Home Edition.* How do they build a home in seven days? Are they skipping steps and cutting corners? No, they're doing everything required to build a home. They're just doing it all at the same time. When the roof is going on, the plumbing is going in. When the drywall is going up, the floors are being laid. It is an amazing thing to watch. It's also the exact opposite of how most homes are built, especially mine. First came the foundation people, then the framers, the electrician and then, eventually, the plumber. The labor time was the same as an *Extreme Makeover* project, but it was dragged out, sequentially, for an eternity.

When my wife and I interviewed the builder from *Extreme Makeover,* I just had to ask to see the project plan for the home he had built in seven days. He took me back to his office, and for me this was like viewing the Mona Lisa. There on his wall was a replica of the project plan he had used for the TV build job. Every task on that project plan was perfectly interlaced. There was no downtime, no white space between tasks. They had built a house in seven days using one simple tool — planning — and one key concept — simultaneous processing.

The idea of simultaneous processing is also the inspiration for the top-selling kitchen gadget of the past decade: the George Foreman grill. Prior to the Foreman grill, cooking a hamburger was a two-step, fourteen-minute process. Cook one side of the burger for seven minutes, then flip it over and cook the other side for another seven minutes. George Foreman comes along and says, "I'm hungry. I can't wait fourteen minutes." Voila, the Foreman grill is born. The concept is so simple: one grill on top, one below. Cooking a burger on it takes half the time. But the work time is still the same. The burger still gets cooked seven minutes per side. The sides are just being grilled in parallel. Compare that to microwaving: Have you ever tried to microwave a hamburger? You only try it once. It's some nasty meat. Microwaving a hamburger is an example of rushing, or trying to cut actual work time. If you rush the work time you end up with bad quality. It's impossible to have a delicious hamburger in less than seven minutes per side. But we can do both sides at the same time.

(What's really frustrating is that I do this stuff for a living and I didn't think of this. George Foreman got hit in the head for twenty-five years and made over $100 million off this! The tactics in this chapter are universal.)

A less pithy example of simultaneous processing is in the area of child welfare. Protecting children is one of the most important things government does, but unfortunately the child protection pipe is also one of the most overburdened systems we have nationwide. Kids who are victims of abuse are often removed from their homes. They then enter a three- to four-year pipe before they're placed in a permanent home again. For the first eighteen months, the court — rightly so — mandates that the child welfare department try to reconcile the child with her original family. If that doesn't work, the court then authorizes the department to begin the adoption process. Astute departments have begun applying the George Foreman grill concept to this process. Using what they call "concurrent planning" (and what we call simultaneous processing), these departments begin much of the adoption work — background checks, suitability interviews, home inspections — at the same time they're working to reconcile the original family. If the reconciliation doesn't happen, these departments are often years ahead of the curve. Departments using this tactic are cutting time-to-permanency in half. What if the family reconciles? Hasn't the agency wasted a lot of work? It has. But what is the purpose of the system? To find safe, suitable homes for children as quickly as possible.

One of the most common pushbacks I get from people when I talk about going faster is that the constraints are out of their hands. Maybe there's a mandatory public comment period of forty-five days, or maybe there's a one-month wait for board approval.

Whatever it is, progress stops and the water sits in the pipe until this timeframe is met. What we often fail to realize, though, is that we could be doing some downstream things during that waiting period. For example, it is good practice to wait until the roof is on before affixing gutters. Typical contractors will wait until the whole roof is on before they call the gutter guys. How does *Extreme Makeover: Home Edition* do it? The gutter guys follow behind the roofers. When one big section of the roof is finished, the gutters go on. And so on. Carpet gets laid as each room is finished, rather than waiting until the whole house is ready. We should always be looking for ways to move downstream activities upstream, which shortens the pipe.

Strategy #3: Bust Your Bottleneck

If you go back to our visual of the pipe, the bottleneck would be a section of the pipe that is thinner than the other sections. The segments before and after the bottleneck are wider and have more capacity than the bottleneck. Consequently, water pressure backs up in front of the bottleneck, and the pipes dry out after it. The productivity of the pipe depends totally on the capacity of the bottleneck.

In other words, you're only as good as your weakest link. This is one of the single most critical things to understand about improving performance, and it is the least understood in the public sector. Results come from the pipes. The problem is capacity. The capacity is determined by your bottleneck. Improving government is not about fixing all of government. It is so much more focused than that. All you have to fix is the bottleneck of the critical pipes. In your whole agency,

I'd bet there aren't more than five places that are kinking your pipes.

So how do you find your bottleneck? The simplest way is to go out and look for it. Put your waders on and find the puddles. In front of every bottleneck there's usually a pile. It can be physical (stacks of paper, rows of file cabinets, overflowing inboxes) or virtual (a pending file, a queueing system, a workflow management system). Oftentimes it can be as simple as looking in the mirror. Are you the bottleneck? Are there people constantly waiting on you to decide, to sign off, or to answer? Do you let things linger in your inbox until you have a full day to tackle them?

I once was conducting a workshop with the administrative division of a large county in the Southwest. During the workshop, the employees drew the pipes of their agency, and I asked them to circle where the biggest gap between work time and elapsed time occurred. For five out of the six processes of that agency, the biggest gap centered on one person: the new CFO. He was the bottleneck in procurement, hiring, payroll, IT prioritization, and other processes. Essentially, he had brought the organization to a standstill. Of course the new CFO was too busy to come to the workshop, but he did pop in at lunch to see what the employees had been up to. As he walked around the room and studied the drawings, he couldn't help but notice the bottlenecks circled in bright red marker. After his tour of the room, he asked if he could address the group after lunch. I had no idea what was coming, and boy was I surprised. When the group reconvened, he praised them for their efforts and then proceeded to apologize to all of them for the damage he had done to their systems. People's jaws hit the floors. He said, "I thought I was doing my job. I thought I was helping. But clearly all I've been doing is slowing everybody down, and I'm sorry." Then came the really cool part. He said, "I have some legitimate reasons why I inserted myself in the process, but there is no reason why we can't accomplish those same things without my involvement." And then the group proceeded to work with him on how to allay his concerns about quality and fiscal priorities while not slowing down the process. That was a great day.

The other simple way to find your bottlenecks is to look where people are quitting. There is a strong correlation between bottlenecks and turnover. Why? Pressure. Water pressure builds up in front of a bottleneck, and so does organizational pressure. For the people who work in a bottleneck unit, their lives are hell. Not because they themselves are slow, but because, by the design of the system, they have less capacity than what is required for things to flow. Consequently, people downstream are constantly hassling them about delays, while people upstream keep flowing more and more work to them. Bottleneck employees feel like they're always in a rush. And they are. And what do most organizations do to relieve the pressure on bottlenecks? They try to "manage" them. And by manage I don't mean help. They get more measures. More reporting. More status updates. More activity targets. More one-on-one personal development. More accountability, which just means more CYA and less capacity. Which of course puts them on the crazy cycle. You want to help a bottleneck? First get rid of all that stuff and see where you are.

How can you eliminate the bottleneck? Start thinking like a traffic engineer. We often associate bottlenecks with traffic jams: Whenever three lanes turn into two lanes, we get a backup. The two-lane road just doesn't have the capacity that the three-lane section did. The obvious solution is to knock down some trees and lay some asphalt. In our world, that would be the equivalent of adding staff, an option that is not typically available to us. The next most obvious answer is to get rid of the cars, to divert the traffic. Try to find as many ways as possible to move work away from the bottleneck. Does everything have to go through legal? Does the division director really have to sign off on every report? We may find alternate roads for some of the workload (often the more routine work), which reduces the work flow for the bottleneck, allowing that unit to focus only on the work that absolutely must go through it.

Sometimes you will discover that you can't get around the bottleneck, but perhaps you can reduce the amount of work required by the bottleneck. One agency I worked with suffered a major bottleneck with its general counsel. In talking with her, she showed me the volumes of documents she had to sift through in order to approve each permit request that came across her desk. My team collaborated with her, and we developed a summary document that pulled all that relevant info out for her into one easy-to-read place. What before had languished on her desk for a month was now approved in a couple of days. It took a ton of work off her and let her do what she was paid to do — read and decide. Did it add extra work on someone else? Yep. But that person wasn't the bottleneck and wasn't paid like a general counsel.

As in that example, what you'll typically find is that the bottleneck is a specialist. That is, he or she is the only one qualified or designated to perform a given task. This can often be statutory: An engineer has to approve a plan, a licensed psychologist must sign off on an evaluation, and so forth. Because they are specialists, it is absolutely critical that they only do specialist work. An attorney shouldn't be concerned with checking a report's grammar, for example. Any portion of the work that could be done by someone else should be done by someone else.

This approach is revolutionizing social service agencies in some governments. Under the old model, a family was assigned a single caseworker who handled all their needs. When caseloads were small, it worked well. But a family's success was dependent on the talents and availability of its caseworker; as more and more work was piled onto the caseworkers, they unwittingly became the bottleneck of the social service system. The solution? Rather than viewing social work as one long pipe, think of the job as a *series* of pipes that must work well. Instead of "casework" we have intake, interview, documentation gathering, eligibility determination, and issuance. The water that leaves one pipe becomes the input for the next pipe. When each pipe is straight and well-managed, the social work case can flow quickly through each pipe to completion. Using data, management can see which pipes are full and move resources to them. Under this new approach, precious caseworker capacity is utilized only in places where that specialty is required. Clerical tasks can be done by clerical staff. Management tasks can be done by management staff. Caseworkers do what caseworkers should do, and want to do: work with clients to diagnose their needs and find the right resources. The results have been staggering: As much as 40 percent more customers served, 70 percent faster, with half as many errors and at half the cost — with no new technology and no new staff.

But hang on a minute. Isn't this the exact opposite of what we talked about in Chapter 5? Haven't we just chopped up the work and created more handoffs?

Yep, that's right. This is the exact opposite of what I usually preach, which is to minimize handoffs, eliminate specialization and do the work as fast as possible with as few hands as possible. But that all falls apart when you have a bottleneck. When your system constraint is a bottleneck, you must do whatever you can to increase the capacity of that bottleneck.

Strategy #4: Quit Your Batching

Imagine you've just begun a vacation. It's been a long flight and you're a little tired, but you're eagerly anticipating the good times ahead. After you've grabbed your luggage and dragged it outside to the curb, you are faced with a choice as to how best get to your hotel. Option 1 is the royal blue Super Shuttle; Option 2, a taxi cab. Remember, this money is coming out of your wallet, not the taxpayers'

When to Add Staff

Budget cuts absolutely cripple agency performance because they are typically done across the board. Everybody loses 10 percent of the staff. What most management and budget folks fail to understand, though, is the simple performance equation. Results come from pipes. Pipes lack capacity. Capacity is determined by the bottleneck. Reducing staff in the bottleneck is counterproductive. It will create more work, thanks to the crazy cycle. During tough budget times, the bottlenecks need to be left alone. When budgets get better, and if we have the ability to hire more people, start in the bottleneck.

pockets. Which option do you take?

If you're like my workshop participants, there's a 90 percent chance you picked the taxi cab, even though it is two to three times more expensive. Adam Smith would be extremely disappointed in you. Our entire economy is predicated on you making rational decisions in your self-interest. So why not take the more economical Super Shuttle? Because we learn from our mistakes.

My first (and last) Super Shuttle experience went a little like this: I was the first one to board the shuttle, and after about five minutes I noticed the driver didn't seem to be interested in going anywhere. I kindly asked her, "Will we be leaving soon?" Her laughter foreshadowed the adventure to come.

She said, "Is this your first time? We don't leave until the van is full."

Ouch. Sure enough, once the van was full (and then what had to be illegally full), we embarked. I then learned the Universal Law of Super Shuttles: First one in, last one out. After an hour of seeing where all my sweaty travel mates were staying, I finally reached my destination and swore to never go through that experience again.

Why do we hate the Super Shuttle? Because it's batch processing. Batch processing holds one customer hostage to a larger group. Batches can be quantity-based or time-based. A quantity-based batch would be something like waiting until we have 100 applications before we send them on to the next unit to be reviewed. A time-based batch would be, say, a policy to only process payments on the third Thursday of the month. In either case, the customer does not flow smoothly through the pipe. Instead, he has to wait. Your hatred for the Super Shuttle is equal to your customers' hatred of batching.

If we go back to our pipe analogy, you can visualize the effects of batching. Without batching, a drop of water — a case, an application, a document — moves through the pipe at its own pace. With a batch, we're essentially adding a dam mechanism into the pipe: Water gets stopped until the level rises to a certain point. Then all that water floods into the next section of the pipe at the same time, which often creates backlog. Again, we have sitting water with all of its side effects: phone calls, tracking mechanisms, expediting, and so on. In an effort to save work, we create work.

Once you start looking for batches in your agency, you'll be amazed at how many you find. The board meets once a quarter. Deposits are posted at 3 p.m. Work requests are assigned to maintenance crews in the morning. The policy review committee meets on Thursday. We wait until we have twenty-five applicants before we send the resumes to the hiring manager. Everywhere, water is sitting in puddles waiting for some arbitrary limit to pass.

So if batches are so odious, why do we do them? Well, because from the agency perspective, they're more convenient.

I'll give you an example. In our house, my wife does the laundry. (Don't worry; I do other chores, just not the laundry.) And with the laundry, she batch-processes. That is, she either waits until the basket is full (a quantity-based batch) or until Saturday morning (a time-based batch), whichever comes first. From her perspective, this is obviously more convenient, not to mention more environmentally friendly. She wouldn't want to do laundry with each dirty shirt or stinky sock. It makes far more sense to her to wait and wash everything at one time. But from the perspective of the "customer" (not that I would ever consider myself a customer in the relationship), the service is a little spotty. If I turn in my shirt in on Friday, great! A one-day turnaround! But if I turn it in on Sunday, it's an awful, six-day turnaround. So is the batching bad? Depends on who you ask. Batching is almost always more convenient from the producer's perspective. And it is almost always less convenient from the customer's perspective. So the caveat about all this batch bashing is simply this: If your batching does not negatively impact your customers, then by all means keep doing it. But if it does negatively impact your customers, then it's time to think of some new options.

The other reason we batch-process goes back to mold, CYA, and control. Call it the field-trip policy: Everyone must stay together. If you can remember your elementary school field trips to the Bee Farm or Pioneer Days or wherever, you remember that everyone must get on the bus together (count heads). Everyone gets off the bus (count heads). If one person has to go the bathroom, everyone goes (count heads). If you want to climb the world's third largest pile of beetle dung, you have to wait until everyone is ready to climb the world's third largest pile of beetle dung (count heads). It's a lot of extra work, a lot of sitting around, and a ton of whining. Why? Fear of losing a kid. Which is a big deal. But fear of losing a document? Not so much.

So what's the alternative to batches? Simple. Just say to yourself, "Batches? We don't need no stinking batches." Seriously, wherever possible, just get rid of them. Let the water flow. If the board only meets once a quarter, what about a more frequent conference call to handle certain decisions? Can we assign work requests the moment they come in? When completely eliminating the batch isn't

A Back-Breaking Batch

There's been much hue and cry in recent years about the growing size of children's backpacks. My own kids' backpacks can easily knock out a large attacker. What's causing these children to slump over? Their textbooks. Because of school violence, many schools have minimized locker use. Instead, every day, each kid is lugging five or six forty-pound books back and forth from home. Well-meaning people have proposed solutions to this posture crisis, and of course one state tried to pass a law about the maximum weight for school books. None of them worked. What's the best solution? Quit your batching. School books are a great example of a batch. Children only need the part of the book they're currently using — ten to 20 pages, tops. Unfortunately, the children are carrying their past and their future around with them. They are dragging around all the pages they've already used, as well as the pages they won't be reading for months to come. The innovative solution has been to break down textbooks into smaller modules. Rather than one big book for social studies, you may have eight small booklets. Ingenious!

an option, consider cutting the batch size in half. If the Super Shuttle only sat seven people instead of fourteen, I'd get to my hotel twice as fast. If the laundry basket was smaller, I'd get my shirt back more quickly. If you process payments once a month, do it twice a

Random Optimization

I once consulted with the management of a mail-order company. It was a really simple operation: Customers looked at a catalog, called in their orders, and the stuff was shipped to them. The organization had basically two divisions: the phone operators who took the orders and the "pickers" who filled the orders from the shelves and prepared the boxes for shipping. The head of the phone operators was new to the company but a seasoned phone-center manager. He measured and improved talk time, hold time, and abandoned calls. For him, the phone-center operation was about one thing: Get off the phone and get the order in the out-basket in seven minutes or less. He tyrannically managed that seven-minute number — posting charts of who was over or under, rewarding the "outstanding performers" and shaming the "chatty" ones. The operators' compensation was all tied to that seven-minute target.

Ready for the punch line? The pickers came and pulled the orders from the out-baskets twice a day, because there were only two shipments per day. Unless UPS was going to show up every seven minutes, that phone-center dictator was oppressing his people for nothing.

month. Then cut the batches in half again. Every time we cut them in half, we go 50 percent faster! Then cut them again and again, until you have the ideal batch size: one. You have a taxi cab.

Strategy # 5: Eliminate Backlog

Remember the moral of the crazy cycle from the Fable of Complexity? Backlog can be one of our biggest time bandits. In fact, quite often in government, the problem isn't that we're slow. It's that we're behind.

So what's the key to avoiding backlog? How can you ensure that you never get behind? Here's the answer: The secret to dealing with backlog is to never get behind in the first place. (Send all thank-you emails to ken@changeagents.info.) Underwhelmed? Well, let's look at this pearl of wisdom a little more closely.

The time I spent managing DMV offices almost led me to believe that it's impossible to design a system that never falls behind. The DMV is actually a great case study of the effects of backlog; you can literally watch the effects of falling a little behind manifest themselves every day. An office can open at 8 a.m., fall a little behind by 9:15, and by noon there are fifty angry people standing in line. The reason this happens with DMV offices actually has nothing to do with the productivity of the employees. It's a function of random variation. At DMV offices (or food stamp offices or public-assistance offices), the number of customers who show up at any one time is completely random. With the exception of lunchtime, there's no rhyme or reason. There is as much probability of four people showing up as forty. If four people arrive at the same time, the office is fine. But if forty people show up at once, the game is over and the office is wrecked for the rest of the day. It seemed like an unavoidable problem, and one without a solution.

But then I learned something from McDonald's. Fast-food restaurants also have the same problem of unpredictable customer patterns, with the obvious exception of mealtimes. That is, there is as much a chance of two customers walking in as twenty. If you've ever been at McDonald's when a bus full of customers shows up, then you have seen the chain's very sophisticated process for dealing with this. It's called "BUS!" That is, when a bus is spotted rolling into the parking lot, an employee screams "BUS!" and the entire restaurant is transformed. Managers and supervisors stop what they're doing and double-man the counters. Cooks start making popular items as fast as they can. All hands are on deck to get the line of customers served as quickly as possible — because if they don't, the lines will be with them all day long. The whole day will be wrecked.

Armed with this insight, we created a "bus" process for the DMVs. Whenever a large group of customers all showed up at once, the entire office transformed. The managers came out of their offices and double-manned the counters. Back-office paperwork specialists came out to work the lines. Everybody pitched in until the line was gone, and then they went back to their regular jobs. It was an amazing thing to watch as everybody cooperated with each other. It was hard work, but the benefits were astounding. By not getting a little bit behind, they never got a lot behind. And life in the office got a lot better.

Designing processes so that you never fall behind requires a whole new way of thinking. In government we tend to practice the ancient art of annual management. That is, we have our annual budget and our annual FTE counts, and that's about all the thought we put into staffing. Unfortunately, our customers don't cooperate by spacing themselves out evenly throughout the day, month, or year. We have fluid customers but static staffing. To avoid ever falling behind, you actually have to manage more actively. For DMV or public-assistance offices, this can be a minute-by-minute battle. For licensing and permitting offices, this may be a week-by-week battle. It also means that you have to cross-train your employees so they can step in to help during high-traffic times. Sound like a lot of management? It is. But not as much management as it takes to handle the call centers, the tracking systems, and the ever-growing pile of documents you get from backlog.

It's one thing to commit to never getting backlogged from now on, but how can you get rid of the backlog you already have now? To tackle the existing backlog in your agency, you need to understand the three different kinds of backlog. The first is historic backlog. In that case, the backlog pile may be sizeable, but it's not growing. For example, every month there may be a pile of roughly 200 cases that don't get handled. Its size fluctuates around a mean. What this tells you is that the process is actually fine — it can keep up. Roughly 400 cases come in to the pipe every month, and 400 exit the pipe every month. It's just not the same 400. With historic backlog, something happened in the past — a hiring freeze, a technology glitch — that got the organization behind. Now everything that comes in gets put on the bottom of the pile and waits. So what do you do to get out of this situation? Grab a shovel and dig out. Hire some temps, borrow some resources, or put in some overtime. Dig out. Do whatever it takes to get rid of that pile. Once it's gone, it is smooth sailing through the pipe.

The second kind of backlog is known as ongoing or growing backlog, and it's trickier. In this case, the pile is growing progressively larger, and the agency is falling further and further behind every month. The system doesn't have the capacity to keep up. What's the solution here? Fix the process. Employ the fast-government techniques I've been describing to increase capacity. Design a process that can handle the workload and then stick to it.

The third kind of backlog is seasonal. All I will say about that is that you know it's coming. It happens the same time every year. So what are you doing to get ready for it?

When you're able to apply these five strategies to your agency — setting up triage, engaging in simultaneous processing, busting bottlenecks, banishing batches, and ending backlog — you can make government run faster. Much faster. But that's only one part of the "Better Faster Cheaper" goal I mentioned at the beginning of this chapter. Going faster is the necessary first step. But we've also got to make government run better. In the next chapter I'll show you how going faster also accomplishes that as well.

Faster on Your Own

"But what if we don't have a pipe? What if there are no handoffs, no big production? What if it's just me?" This is a question I get frequently. In this Knowledge Age, a lot of us don't mass-produce large volumes of widgets. We custom-produce one widget at a time. For many of us, our widgets are policies, directions, or answers. We're providing technical assistance or helping people find information. How does all this stuff about kinked-up pipes and batches, specialization, and bottlenecks apply to us?

The important things to keep in mind are the universal concepts of elapsed time and work time. The gap may not be the same 95 percent as for large, complex pipes. But it's still significant. Tasks clog our pipes and create pressure. We feel rushed, harried, disorganized. Just like the pipes, our brain is deluged. And just like the pipes, the only way to get more done is to go faster.

The solutions for fixing our own personal task factories are similar to those we use to straighten pipes in an organization:

1. Cut the elapsed time and do just the work. Veteran management consultant David Allen, in his book *Getting Things Done: The Art of Stress-Free Productivity,* suggests the two-minute rule. If you can finish a task in two minutes or less, do it immediately. If you can't, then schedule the task.

2. Eliminate backlog. You'll always be in the mental crazy cycle if you don't get rid of your backlog. Each new request will get piled on top all the other emails you haven't answered, leading to the constant anxiety that you're missing something. Just like with the pipes, you have to get rid of the historical backlog and institute a "bus" policy so you never get behind again.

3. Bust the bottleneck. Treat yourself as a specialist — only focus on the things you yourself need to handle. If you have more tasks coming in than going out, you need to find a way to delegate.

4. Triage. Most of us don't triage what comes in. It all goes in the same inbox. We need to quickly route requests of us to their appropriate places so we don't have to keep tracking them. Allen suggests three pathways for incoming info. Complete it within two minutes, schedule it for later, or discard it completely.

For many of us, our own personal pipes are part of larger pipes called projects. The project is the factory of the Knowledge Age. Many of us spend most of our time stuck in these new project factories. And the factories are a mess.

Contrary to the teachings of the Project Management Body of Knowledge (and its certification process and reams of CYA), projects aren't late because we use the wrong Gantt chart. Projects are late for the same reasons our processes are so bad: They're too slow. We don't need better project management, we need project *improvement,* using the same principles we use for agencies. Do tasks in parallel, bust bottlenecks. The path of a project should be a short, straight pipe.

What really causes projects to be late, however, and what most project management methods don't account for, is natural human behavior. Let's say you've been assigned a key task on a project. The project manager says, "I'm building the schedule and need to know how much time it will take you to finish your task." Let's say it will take you eight hours. But you know there's little chance you'll have that dedicated time. So you reply, "Two weeks." See what you just did? And it's not just you. Everyone on the project does the exact same thing. The estimated complete date is usually about 80 percent beyond the sum of the work time. Sound familiar?

But that's only half the problem. There's another human behavior malady that kicks in. It's what management guru Eli Goldratt calls "the student syndrome." When do most students finish their homework? The night before it is due. When will we finish the task we've been assigned in the project? The night before. This is also known as Parkinson's Law: Work expands to fill the amount of time allotted for it.

The danger with Parkinson's Law is a different law: Murphy's Law, which states that anything that can go wrong will go wrong. My computer gets a virus, my kid breaks his arm, the network is down. All conspire to ruin my eleventh-hour workathon. I'll be late. And so will everyone after me.

The student syndrome, Murphy, Parkinson, batching, bottlenecks, backlog — the culprits that clog up all pipes.

Improvement in organizations happens at three levels:

• The organization is trying to get more initiatives done: It needs to increase its capacity to do more projects.

• The systems are trying to get more widgets done: They need to increase the capacity of their pipes (processes).

• The individuals are trying to get more tasks done: They need to increase the capacity of their days.

Projects, processes, and people. These are the pipes through which everything gets done. All three share the same problem (capacity) and the same solutions (cutting elapsed time and focusing on work time).

CHAPTER 7

Better

If you watch a few episodes of *Extreme Makeover: Home Edition,* there's one thing that you'll notice pretty quickly. The houses they build aren't shacks. They're actually quite impressive. The high-quality homes are built to meet all the right municipal codes and standards. They have roofs, multiple stories, gutters and usually a dozen flat-screen TVs scattered throughout. It's not as if the builders get to the big reveal at the end of the episode and say, "We only had seven days! You didn't really expect us to put in windows, did you?"

When I talk to people about making government go 80 percent faster, the first question they throw back at me is whether quality will suffer. Won't going faster make our work sloppier?

Absolutely not. I am not advocating cutting corners. It's not about skipping the windows or leaving off the gutters. Is *Extreme Makeover* doing fourteen months of work in seven days? No. They are doing seven days of work in seven days. The way we go 80 percent faster is not by doing the tasks themselves faster, but by radically rethinking the system so that we're just doing the tasks — only the tasks — with as little lost time as possible between them.

The Principle of One

Most people who have seen *Extreme Makeover* think that the reason the show can build a house in seven days is because of the 300 volunteer laborers. In reality, those volunteers usually end up doing non-critical work, moving materials, getting food, and so forth. The essence of the house-building is still done by the pros. The reason they can build a home in seven days is because they are building just one home. The reason my home took fourteen months was because the builder was also building five other homes at the same time. The carpenter, plumber, and finishing guy kept getting moved from job to job as the builder dictated. The carpenter would start in a room and then disappear for a few weeks. To us, it looked like he wasn't doing anything. The reality was that he was working somewhere else. Progress on our home was continuously tied to progress on the other homes. Even though our home was started five months before the others, we all finished at about the same time.

Working on five homes at once is multitasking. The builder was trying to keep five customers happy by making a little progress on each home. The opposite of multitasking is what I call the Principle of One, or what manufacturing now refers to as "single-piece flow." In essence, you ask, "How long would it take to produce just one of these widgets? If this was all you had to do, and you only had to do one, how long would it take?" This question strips away all of the system stuff and gets right back to the work time. If you only had to produce one widget, you wouldn't batch it, track it, inventory it, expedite it, answer calls about it, and on and on. Our pipes have become so kinked and twisted over the years that many of us can't remember what the actual work is and what is CYA. The Principle of One is the magic question: If we just had one of these to do, how long would it take? The answer for building a home is seven days.

You will note that this is fundamentally different from what we are typically taught. Most process improvement efforts start with a detailed flowchart capturing infinitesimal levels of minutiae. The work group then sets about the hard task of protecting their territory against constant verbal assaults of, "Why do you do it that way?" Eventually, each person begins to sound like my Harley-riding friend from the previous chapter, vociferously explaining why we don't understand what they go through. The whole thing dissolves into a playground squabble of hurt feelings and a meaningless report detailing how they will make a 2 or 3 percent improvement.

There is no quicker way to get a black eye or a bloody nose than telling an attorney, an engineer, or a nurse how to do their jobs differently. It doesn't have to be this way. We can improve by 80 percent without even bothering with what these folks are actually doing. The 95/5 time ratio makes no distinction about what is "value added" and what is not. All of the tasks — value-added or not — add up to less than 5 percent of the total time. You *really* want a black eye? Tell someone that what they are doing adds no value. You can go there if you want to, but I promise you the biggest opportunities are not in the tasks themselves. They are in the system in which the tasks reside, and in the policies and procedures that make seemingly non-value-added work entirely necessary.

Let me be absolutely clear: I am not talking about rushing or expediting. We get more done by straightening the pipes, not shoving the water through. Attempts to make tasks faster lead to sloppy, shoddy work. And in the critical business of government, this can lead to great tragedy. When, say, nursing home inspectors rush their investigations, deficiencies go unnoticed and seniors get hurt. But when the system of nursing home licensure — from law to license to inspection — is streamlined, then capacity increases dramatically and investigators can take the time to do comprehensive work and build more constructive relationships with the facility management.

Or think about home visits for child-abuse calls. We don't want the social workers rushing through their tasks. When the broken system has them responding to way more calls than they possibly can handle, this is exactly what happens — and children get hurt. When the system — from the hotline call to the dispatch to the investigation, documentation, and court processes — is redesigned, capacity dramatically increases and social workers can spend more time with the family.

When we rush, bridges collapse, buildings fall down, oil wells leak, Martha doesn't get paid, and I show up at church with one blue sock and one black one.

We rush because our pipes don't have the capacity they need. Straightening the pipes — going faster — doesn't hurt quality. It does just the opposite. Increased capacity gives us the time to do the quality work we expect of ourselves.

Poka yoke

The other reason why I can boldly proclaim that we can do the vital work of government 80 percent faster without compromising quality is a simple concept called *poka yoke*. It's a Japanese term commonly translated as "mistake-proof" or "idiot-proof." I prefer "idiot-proof" because I'm usually the one these fail-safe measures were created for. For example, my new car won't let me lock the keys inside it the way my old one would. If the key is inside the car, the doors won't lock. I can't leave my gas cap at the gas station because it's tethered to the fuel door. At home, my bathroom sink won't overflow either, despite my best attempts. I typically turn it on and, while waiting for the water to heat up before I shave, I go catch a little *SportsCenter*. In my old home without the sink overflow hole, I would be sopping up water for hours. *Poka yoke* is the automatic shut-off function on my iron. It's the pop-up thermometer in my Thanksgiving turkey.

McDonald's is filled with *poka yoke* techniques. McDonald's has an interesting workforce challenge. The restaurant chain could try to recruit and retain the best and the brightest, in which case hamburgers would cost twelve bucks apiece. Or they can try to keep hamburgers at sixty-nine cents. To have cheap hamburgers, they have cheap labor. Unfortunately those workers aren't always paying attention. So how do you get consistent, "quality" hamburgers from a workforce that isn't paying attention? *Poka yoke.* When are the French fries done at McDonald's? When the buzzer goes off. There's not a single kid in that restaurant kitchen who knows how to make a French fry. They don't know how long to cook them or at what temperature. All they know is that to make that annoying buzzer stop, they have to hit that red button. Heck, the fries even rise out of the oil automatically. Idiot-proof.

McDonald's has also taken a similar tack with its cash registers. If you've ever glanced at them, you've seen that they have pictures on them. Cheeseburger, fries, shake — you can't mess it up. McDonald's has idiot-proofed the registers so much, in fact, that in some test-markets they've tried turning the register around so that it faces the customer. Now the real "idiots" in the restaurant can walk up, push the buttons of what they want, swipe their card, and wait for the food.

Sticking with restaurants for a moment (can you tell I eat out a lot?), Chipotle offers another example of the divergent approaches to making mistakes. Chipotle, for those who may not be connoisseurs of low-priced Mexican fare, is a chain famous for its enormous burritos. These artery assassins come served in foil and placed in a red basket. The idea is that you eat the burrito and leave the basket with Chipotle. Apparently, nationwide, idiots like me continue to throw our baskets away. So throughout the restaurant, there are signs that read, "Please Do Not Discard Your Baskets." It's even stenciled above the trash can. I know this because I read it just after I've accidentally thrown my basket in the trash. Every single time.

Contrast that with a sandwich shop I frequent, Quiznos, which serves its delicious toasty treats on a tray shaped liked a Q. Like Chipotle, Quiznos would like to have the tray back at the end of the meal. But unlike Chipotle, there are no annoying signs reminding me not to be an idiot. Instead, the hole for the trash can is half the size of the tray. Every time I go to throw my tray away, it bounces back up, hits me in the chest and I say, "Oh, dummy, don't throw your tray away." Idiot-proof.

Government tends to follow the Chipotle model. We discover a problem and we create a policy. We then communicate the policy. When that doesn't work, we communicate it again and again, louder and with more emphasis. We usually follow that up with sessions to educate the public that no one attends. What the purveyors of *poka yoke* get, and what we in government don't, is that you can't change customer behavior. No policies or campaigns or trainings will change what people do. So make the hole smaller. Rather than trying to change everyone else, change you.

One of the best examples I've ever seen showed up back when I was helping improve wait times at DMV offices. Now, one of the biggest sources of water into the pipes — at DMVs and at lots of other government offices — is repeat customers. In a typical DMV office, up to half the people in line are there on their second, third, or fourth attempt. Despite all the letters the state mailed explaining what to bring in, despite detailed lists on the website and the huge signs in the lobby, customers inevitably would forget to bring all the necessary documents. For the DMV offices I was working with, the customer service model had amounted to "Too Bad For You." Customers were told to go home, get the right documents, and come back again later. In fact, our stats showed that six in ten customers were being sent away. When they would return (angry and frustrated), they'd clog the line and rob us of capacity.

We worked with the managers to shift from a "Too Bad For You" approach to a "How Can We Help?" model. For instance, the most common reason customers were being turned away was for failing to bring proof-of-insurance documentation. For lots of people, myself included, locating an insurance card is a fool's errand. It's just not gonna happen. So under the new management approach, no customer was sent home until we'd done everything we could to find the right information for them. In most cases, this involved having the customer move out of the line while somebody contacted the insurance carrier and had the card faxed over. This worked, but it required a lot of effort. Finally, the management built relationships with all of the major insurance providers to get electronic access to their policy lists. They did the same thing with county tax collectors, because the second most frequently forgotten item was a proof that you had paid your property taxes. Now, someone like me can walk into the office completely oblivious of my civic duty and walk out with a shiny set of plates. These measures led to more than a 50 percent reduction in repeat visitors.

The same problem of missing documentation plagues the nation's public assistance offices. Increased CYA measures to reduce "fraud" have led to increasingly complicated documentation requests. (Could *you* produce your last three pay stubs or the receipts for your last six months' rent?) Lots of governments are working to change their policies and regulations in order to simplify these requirements without compromising the integrity of their work. But inevitably, customers still don't have what they need when they show up for food or health assistance. The typical approach would be to explain in great detail, often with a translator, what the person needs to bring in next time. If the office was feeling really "helpful," they'd hand the customer a copy of the regulations. What happened next? The customers still brought in the wrong stuff or failed to bring anything.

In public assistance offices, my team has worked with to *poka yoke,* customers who have to go home to get more documents are handed a piece of paper for each document. The papers show exactly what the document looks like — with pictures — along with step-by-step instructions for how to get it and support numbers if any questions arise. Repeat visits dropped dramatically.

Again, many adopt the approach that it's the customers' responsibility to comply with the laws and regulations. (Of course, these are also the same people who will refuse to call them "customers.") They view the myriad of requirements as some kind of gauntlet that people need to run in order to "earn" what they're trying to obtain. That viewpoint is not only inhumane; it robs us of our most precious resource — our capacity to do more good. If you really want to save money in entitlements, lower the costs of administering them. Straighten the pipes and you can serve more people with the same resources.

The reality is that, when you study your pipes, most of the problems you deal with happen at the very beginning. The very first interface with the customer creates most of the havoc we deal with later on. If a form letter is hard to understand, the customers do the wrong thing. If an application form is too complicated, customers don't fill it out correctly. If the data-entry screens are too complex, the employees don't fill them out completely or accurately. In the book *If We Can Put a Man on the Moon,* management authors John O'Leary and Bill Eggers do a great job of explaining how good legislative intent becomes completely unmanageable operations. If we can idiot-proof the policies, the regs, the applications, and the software, then half of our problems will vanish. Begin at the beginning.

By straightening our pipes, we move people through the system faster. The remarkable thing is that we also do it better. It's better for the customer — shorter waits and fewer frustrations. But it's also better for government. When we're able to help customers right the first time, we're left with more resources to assist the people who really need our help. We increase our capacity to do more good, and that's better government.

We can make government faster, and we can make it better. But the billion dollar question is this: Does that make it cheaper?

Check, Please!

One popular way *poka yoke* manifests itself is checklists: Making a fool-proof catalog of everything that needs to be done. In government, it can save valuable time and money. In other areas, it can save lives.

Checklists and *poka yoke* even inserted themselves into the Washington debate over health-care reform. President Obama circulated an interview with Atul Gawande, a surgeon who has written in *The New Yorker* and elsewhere about how to control runaway health-care costs. His latest book, *The Checklist Manifesto: How to Get Things Right,* discusses how to improve health-care outcomes and reduce medical mistakes by using simple checklists. In the interview circulated by Obama, from Salon.com, Gawande laid out his case:

> What we're grappling with in reform of public health is immense complexity. We do 50 million operations a year in the U.S., with 150,000 deaths within 30 days. Five hundred thousand people are disabled, and half of those are avoidable. When we think about how we grapple with complexity, we've been using two solutions: super-specialization and technology. These haven't been good enough. When I looked at how other worlds like aviation and construction grapple with complexity, I found checklists.

But checklists are also an admission of fallibility. It's an admission that individuals aren't the only thing that matter, that chains of people and processes matter. Further, it's an admission that we can't handle the complexity that's coming at us. And I think that's the case across lots of walks of life.

In a September 2008 article in *McKinsey Quarterly*, called "The Ergonomics of Innovation," one physician discussed how checklists could revolutionize health care in the same way they were used to increase aviation safety half a century ago:

> We are built on a 2,000-year-old culture, where we are expected as clinicians not to make mistakes. This was true with the FAA until the 1950s, when they started asking, "Why are we crashing so many planes?" If your safety systems are built on the expectations that your pilots and your doctors won't fail, then you are going to have no safety net when they do. The FAA figured out pretty quickly that they were better off designing a system that expects the pilots to fail and then prevents that failure from causing a disaster — the failure does not have to cause a disaster. We are just beginning that journey 50 years later in health care. I've gone around asking doctors if they would get on an airplane when a pilot says, "I don't use checklists. I've been doing this for 20 years."

CHAPTER 8

Cheaper

Straightening the pipes makes us faster and, perhaps counter-intuitively, better. Before we talk about how that makes things cheaper — and, trust me, it does — let's take a look at some of the usual cost-saving strategies that governments attempt.

1. Managing the budget. About every two years, the public sector is greeted with a new budget fad: zero-based budgeting, budgeting for results, outcome-based budgeting, the price of government, and on and on and on. They all have slightly different names, with different lead singers, but the songs sound remarkably the same. What they're singing about is a careful, logical, data-driven approach to allocating scarce resources. By deftly explaining each program's purpose, measuring whether it's achieving that purpose, and then calculating the program's cost-benefit ratio, elected officials will abandon all partisanship, ideology, and constituent loyalties and either ax or grow a government program. This is simply not how the budget process works, or will ever work. Elected officials use a lot of things to make their very difficult decisions, but logic and data are not chief among them. At best, all these budget and measurement exercises do is give budget analysts a little more knowledge about the impact of looming budget cuts. At worst, they're giant wastes of time, robbing management of the capacity to actually improve operations. The biggest waste in government is all the stuff we try to do to fight waste in government.

I fully understand why these programs are attractive. I even used to create and sell these defective widgets. They are a thoughtful response to the ugly process of across-the-board budget cuts. Across-the-board cuts are unfair, unthinking, and unfeeling. They actually punish efficiency. Let's say you run a diligent agency that saved a million dollars out of your $10 million budget through operational improvements this year. A 10 percent budget cut next year means 10 percent off your lower, more efficient budget — meaning you've just lost $1.9 million. Your sister agency, meanwhile, didn't save a dime. The 10 percent cut means that agency's only down by $1 million. In other words, that agency has $900,000 more dollars than you just for being inefficient.

Across-the-board cuts just plain suck, but they're not going away. Because the supposed cure — rational, data-driven budgeting — is a myth. It's a legend as rare as a unicorn or a U.S. World Cup soccer championship.

The reason the cure doesn't work isn't because the patient won't take the pill. It's because the cure is based on a misdiagnosis. Government budgets are not chock-full of extraneous programs that are wastefully spending precious resources to achieve outdated policy aims. When you do the calculations, you see that they all actually have a positive ROI. The issue is not that the programs don't work; it's that we don't have enough capacity to do them all enough.

2. Blue ribbon commissions. I took quite a few shots at blue ribbon commissions in *We Don't Make Widgets,* so I won't pile on too much here. A good friend made a mock "Successories" poster for me that I've hung in my office with great pride. It shows a giant can of Pabst Blue Ribbon beer, and the caption reads, "Having a blue ribbon doesn't mean it's good." The very notion of the blue ribbon cost-cutting commission is insulting. Essentially, the elected officials are saying, "We've got no idea where to cut; the budget analysts who pore over this stuff twelve hours a day are out of ideas; and the departments won't cough anything up. So we're going to have a genetically superior private-sector business leader attend four or five meetings and show us how it's done."

It doesn't work. As I point out in *Widgets*, the main reason this approach is doomed to fail is that "they" don't get "us." They come from a world of widgets, factories, customers, and bottom lines. At first blush, it would seem we don't have that stuff (unless you read the book) so they don't see the systems in government. And as I detailed in Chapter 2, when the systems are invisible you reach for what you can see — fleet cars, org charts, print shops, paper clips, and, of course, people. That's why these commissions always produce the same reports: Reorganize, consolidate, automate, and motivate.

We don't need outsiders showing us how to reduce expenses. We need *insiders* showing us where to reduce *costs*. Can an outside perspective be useful? You bet — after we have made the pipes visible. One of the most powerful things you can do, once you've made your system visible, is to go visit other people with similar systems and learn from them. But having a group of outsiders speaking abstractly about operations they can't see gets us nowhere.

3. Contests. I made light of the Obama cost-cutting contest in the opening chapter as proof that we are out of ideas. Let me elaborate on why those contests seldom work, regardless of who is in power. The idea behind these contests is to get around the bureaucracy, the entrenched management team that has supposedly been stifling these great ideas for all these years. By doing an end run around management, supposedly we can hear directly from the workers on the front lines. And what do they tell us? Well, it reminds me of my favorite tweets from "S#*! My Dad Says." (In case you don't know, "S#*! My Dad Says" is a Twitter feed from a guy named Justin Halpern, who moved back home with his parents and decided to tweet the ridiculously caustic and funny pearls of wisdom his aging father would spout at him. It has since become a book and TV show with William Shatner.) Justin's dad, in response to his brother's concern that his baby wasn't talking yet, was this: "The baby will talk when he talks. It's not like he knows the cure for cancer and he just ain't spitting it out."

Your front-line employees don't have the cure for your agency's cancer. It's not because they're not smart enough, or engaged or innovative enough. The problem is their perspective. They're trapped in the system. Worse, they're trapped in small parts of the system. They may see clearly how to make improvements or cut costs in their own small part of the pipe. But that improvement may be inconsequential to the pipe as a whole; sometimes, optimizing performance for one part of the system can sub-optimize performance of the system as a whole.

For example, a very common front-line suggestion is to "give us our own [fill-in-the-blank]." Giving a unit its own IT guy, its own car, or its own customer database absolutely would make that unit more successful. But that may rob the agency of capacity in other areas. Another common suggestion is to allow a unit to move to a four-day, ten-hour-a-day work week. For some, that can be a good idea with no negative impact on the organization or its customers. But what if that unit is the bottleneck? What if water can't flow through the pipe until it goes through your unit, and you're off on Fridays? These are extreme examples, and most front-line suggestions are far more thoughtful than these. But nearly all suffer from the same myopia: You can't improve what you can't see. And most lower-level staff can't see the system. (Most upper-level staff can't see it either, for the same reason: They've been too compartmentalized by the organizational structure.) So how do we best tap into the creativity of front-line employees? Change their perspective. Put them on projects to study the whole pipe and they will not only cure your cancer but give you a tummy-tuck and a full head of hair to boot.

So if the old approaches of government — attacking the budget, forming blue ribbon commissions and hosting contests — don't work, then what does? To answer that question, we must understand what truly drives the cost in government: the systems. Expenses are visible; costs are invisible.

Five Main Cost Drivers

Cost Driver #1: Time. The old adage that time is money couldn't be more accurate for government. The longer something takes, the more it costs. Think back to our discussion of the crazy cycle. When something flows through our system quickly, there is little need to track it, batch it, inspect the handoffs, expedite the bottleneck, and so forth. The longer something stays in our pipes, the more we have to manage it. All that management translates to more costs.

As I mentioned before, customers who get stuck in our pipes rarely just sit there patiently. Instead, they engage what British systems thinker John Seddon refers to as "progress-chasing." Progress-chasing, in the form of constant phone calls and repeat visits, includes:

- "I sent in my application and want to make sure you got it."
- "I haven't heard back from you and wanted to see where we are in the process."
- "I left you a ton of messages and no one will return my calls."
- "Maybe you lost it so I re-sent it."
- "I was afraid you would lose it so I brought it in."
- "Where is my stuff?"
- "Seriously, where's my stuff?"

All of these progress checks cost money and get us further behind. The customers trying to figure out where they are in this clogged-up system

The Management Gap

Five percent of the time that a customer is in our pipes, labor is happening.

Ninety-five percent of the time, management is happening.

are the very ones clogging the system in the first place. The more progress-chasers call, the more employees are required to handle the calls, meaning they get less work done, fall further behind, and start getting more calls. Eventually, we wake up five years later and find that the phone-center staff is now as big as the processing staff and the office is spending $50 million on software that only tells them how far behind they are.

The current approach to handling progress-chasing and the crazy cycle in government is actually exacerbating the problem. In an effort to emulate the private sector and provide "great customer service," we have professionalized and specialized call management. Large centralized call-centers are occupying cubicle farms in public assistance, IT support, employment benefits, social security, child support, and other areas big and small. Layers of management are employed to supervise call-center staff, handle Level 2 calls and explain why the phones never get answered. It's all become a very sophisticated and professional operation. And costly. And completely unnecessary. We have gotten incredibly good at managing what shouldn't exist: calls.

Nearly every phone call we get in the public sector is a defect; that is, it shouldn't have happened. Don't believe me? Go spend an afternoon in your agency's phone center. The vast majority of the calls are either "Where is my stuff?" or "I don't understand." They're defects. Rather than spending more money to log, track, and quality-control these phone calls, we should instead spend more time eliminating the *source* of these calls. Great customer service means never having to call.

When I've worked with call-center managers, the first thing we do is have the call-center staff identify the ten kinds of phone calls they receive most frequently, which usually account for about 80 percent of the total calls. We then map each call back to the pipe that causes it. And what do these exercises reveal? That we have a few pipes that take too long, and a few forms/letters/procedures that no one can understand. We then put call-center staff on the teams formed to straighten the pipes, and we *poka yoke* the forms. Call volume drops immediately.

The solution for dealing with progress-chasing and the crazy cycle is not to get better at managing it, but instead to go so fast that it can't occur! The longer something takes, the more it costs. Conversely, the faster we go, the less it will cost.

Public assistance offices are a great example of the high cost of slow service. The economic downturn has increased demands on these systems by 40 to 50 percent, and the impact has been devastating. The water (that is, the customers) is spilling everywhere, the pipes are bursting, and everyone is freaking out. What is important to understand is that the economic crisis didn't cause these system problems. It amplified them. Standing in the lobby of a public assistance office feels like standing in pool of rising water. It's beyond grabbing a mop or plugging a hole. There is a tidal wave of people all waiting to wait, taking a number to take a number. When we study the reasons people call or visit the office, however, something glaring jumps out. Less than 30 percent of the people are there to get benefits. What are the other 70 percent doing?

Forty percent of them are simply trying to figure out what is taking so long. They are standing in line for hours to figure out where they are in the pipe. Mind you, this is after they have likely called the phone center three, four, or five times. The offices cry out that they need more resources to answer the calls and serve all the people in line. Nope. They just have to go faster and the water quickly recedes.

Let's look at another example of the relationship between time and money. In this case, big money. My team had the great fortune to work with a progressive corrections department at the height of our previous fiscal crisis, in 2001 and 2002. We were knee-deep in a project looking at the parole system when the budget crisis began. The parole system pipe begins months (sometimes years) prior to an inmate's release date and includes a series of milestones that must be met by the prisoner and staff before the inmate can exit the pipe and enter society. If everything happens correctly, the prisoner is released on time. If things slip … well, here's what we found.

Releasing prisoners early is one of the tactics of last resort for governors in tough budget times. It's political suicide. Closing prisons makes enemies in the towns that depend on them for jobs. Letting inmates out early always backfires, as, inevitably, one does something heinous and the governor has to run against that crime in the next election. Our governor at the time was in just such a dilemma, and he had decided to close two prisons and release a large group of nonviolent offenders early. While this decision was being debated, our team analyzed the pipes and found something startling: Thousands of inmates were stuck in the pipes. They had already served their time and were waiting on the parole board (the bottleneck) to send them home. When we did the math across the entire prison system, we had the equivalent of two whole prisons' worth of inmates who should no longer be in our expensive custody. Exactly the amount the governor was poised to release, although not, of course, the same inmates.

Armed with this data, the corrections director and the governor's chief of staff convinced the governor and the legislature that there was a better course of action. Working with the parole board, they implemented a triage system to move the easy cases through more quickly so they could better focus on the serious offenders. Time equals money. The inmates were stuck in the pipes. When we unclogged the pipes and sped the flow out of the system, we saved over $200 million and averted a potential public safety disaster and political nightmare.

The solution to a slow process is to speed up the process. The solution is not to hold the pipes accountable. But that's exactly what concerned, well-meaning elected officials try to do. When a process is taking too long, they insert a mandate with consequences. For example, food assistance cards have to be delivered to customers within thirty days of application. If not, the agency gets fined by the federal government. (Think about that for a second. The pipes don't have the capacity to keep up with all the water, so the solution is to punish them and reduce their capacity. Genius.) On the surface, setting a time limit seems like a good idea. Families should be able to get food stamps within a month. Business should be able to get permits in ninety days. Citizens should be able to get their tax refund before they pay their taxes again. But in practice, here's what really happens: The mandate becomes the new lowest common denominator. Let's say your agency processes permits, on average, in sixty days. A few drag out longer, and unfortunately a vocal few really drag out, for six or nine months. The elected officials, after getting an earful (and a pocketful) from the aggrieved businesses, step in and mandate that no permit can take longer than six months. Guess how long all permits will now take? Six months. Same staff, same resources, same procedures. But now it takes six months instead of sixty days. This is what I call the gravitational pull of legislative standards. As I mentioned in Chapter 6, it's also called Parkinson's Law: Work expands to fill the amount of time allotted for it.

Measuring the pipes, yelling at the pipes, and holding the pipes accountable does not straighten the pipes. The pipes don't listen. Straighten the pipes, speed the flow, lower your costs.

Cost-saving strategy #1: Serve the customer as fast as possible.

Cost Driver #2: Transactions. Transactions are the real cost-drivers in government. Without the customer, no costs are incurred. Every time customers have to interact with us, costs begin — the costs

Assisting Public Assistance

Let's return to our public assistance story. Remember the problem: Forty percent more customers with 20 percent less staff. Added to that was the pressure applied by the federal government that customers receive their benefits within thirty days, or else a severe fine would be levied. How can you serve 40 percent more customers, better, with less money? You have to go faster.

In the offices we worked with, we quickly abandoned the thirty-day goal. The goal was to go as fast as possible. Utilizing the Principle of One, we discovered that each customer required about ninety minutes to two hours of work. Rather than spreading ninety minutes out over thirty days, we decided to do ninety minutes in ninety minutes — essentially giving customers same-day service. When they get their benefits the same day they apply, they don't have a chance to call, and we don't pay any where's-my-stuff tax. In addition, we don't pay the management tax either, as there was little need to track, expedite, and manage the workflow. Customers got their benefits faster, the agency served more customers, quality went up (putting an end to rushing equals better quality). And here's the kicker: The costs per client dropped by 40 percent. The longer something takes, the more it costs. A short, straight pipe can handle more water at less cost.

of serving them, tracking them, corresponding with them, and sympathizing with them. Obviously, some transactions are inevitable. But many are avoidable.

This was the issue we faced with the DMV offices we worked with. The lines were long, but half of the people shouldn't have been there. For them, this was their second, third, or even fourth visit to get the same thing done. Each visit, in addition to adding to the aggravation level, cost us and them time and money. Working with the great staff, we not only tried to get rid of the repeat transactions, we actually found a way to eliminate as many transactions as possible. Our two biggest transactions and cost-drivers were the annual renewal of license plates and the once-every-three-years renewal of drivers' licenses. Why not renew license plates every two years? Why not extend the driver's license renewal to six years instead of three? In both cases, we were told by experts that the upfront expenses would be problematic: Citizens would not want to pay two years of car taxes at once or double their fee for a longer license. So we decided to make it optional, to let the customers choose. With these changes and the advent of online renewals (another way of eliminating transactions), many of our once-clogged offices turned into ghost towns. Eliminating transactions increases capacity and drives down costs.

Phone calls are the most frequent transactions most agencies have with their customers. As I have already discussed, most of these calls are "Where is my stuff?" calls. They didn't get it. What are most of the rest of the calls? "I don't get it." That is, we have sent the customer something and they don't understand what to do next. At most government phone centers, you can see the call volumes spike every time the agency sends out a notice. We ask the customer to do something — pay a delinquency, send in a missing document, renew a license — they don't understand what we are asking of them, and they call.

The state of Washington pioneered a revolution in getting rid of

"I don't get it" calls in 2006, with an initiative called Plain Talk. All critical communication between agencies and citizens would be stripped of bureaucratic doublespeak and legalese, and be rewritten in a way that average citizens could understand. User groups of citizens reviewed correspondence and made recommendations. The results were phenomenal. The Revenue Department, for example, collected an extra $800,000 over two years simply by re-writing one letter. Here is one example of the difference the plain talk initiative made, from the Department of Labor and Industries:

> *Before*: "We have been notified that you did not receive the State of Washington warrant listed on the attached Affidavit of Lost or Destroyed Warrant Request for Replacement, form F242."
>
> *After*: "Have you cashed your L&I check yet? The state Treasurer's Office has informed us that a check we sent you has not been cashed."

"I didn't get it" and "I don't get it" are two of the biggest cost-drivers in government. Make things easier to understand for your customers, and you reduce the number of transactions — along with costs.

> *Cost-saving strategy #2:* Serve the customer in as few visits as possible.

Cost Driver #3: Mistakes. Part of the cost of mistakes is obvious: You have to do the work again. But the true cost goes beyond that. The real cost of mistakes is the CYA they leave in their wake. Someone messes up; they're told to never do it again; so they build in safeguards. But more CYA measures mean less capacity to do the work itself, which leads to more pressure, more rushing, more mistakes.

This cycle is about to play itself out again in the public assistance world. Whenever budgets get really tight, elected officials shift the blame to the customers and the workers by driving out "waste, fraud, and abuse." There is usually some bogus number extrapolated from an egregious case to show how much money is being siphoned. And how do they combat waste, fraud, and abuse? Check, check, and recheck. CYA. The assumption is that more controls will equal better quality. But that idea is based in the old-school world of manufacturing, prior to the quality movement.

The old manufacturing quality model was characterized by the Hanes underwear commercials of the early 1980s. These ads featured a scary-looking lady known only as "Inspector 12." She was shown in the underwear factory at the end of the line twisting underpants and grumbling her tag line, "They don't say Hanes until I say they say Hanes." In the old world of quality, manufacturers ensured customers got a quality product by adding inspectors to the end of the line. Their job was to catch any defects before they got to the customer, and to send the faulty products back to be reworked. The reason Total Quality Management revolutionized the widget world was that it stood this notion on its ear. Catching mistakes at the end of the line is wasteful and expensive. Why not figure out what mistakes are common or possible and prevent them from happening? That is the practice of *poka yoke* I described before.

Unfortunately, we in government are often stuck in the Hanes underwear model. When a mistake happens, we slap on the CYA and add inspectors. We assume that more eyes equal better quality. If five people looked at it and didn't catch it, we'd better add a sixth. This concept was brought home to me in a workshop I once led for a medium-sized county. These officials were looking at five different pipes in the workshop, and one happened to be their IT procurement process. When we actually drew out their procurement process, the awful monstrosity took up two large walls and included no fewer than seven signatures for an employee to buy the most basic of computer needs. (This wasn't even their high-dollar IT procurement process, which, when mapped, would have covered the Great Wall of China.)

It just so happened that all seven signatories were in the room and were dumbfounded by the process. So I asked the first-level sign-off,

Gary, "What do you look at when you sign off on the requisition?"

He said, "Honestly, Ken, there are six people that look at this thing after me. I just sign it and pass it on."

So I asked his boss, "What do you look at when you sign it?"

He said, "Well, I figure if anybody knows better whether the employee needs the stuff or not, it's Gary. So if he's signed it, I sign it."

And on we went up the chain and they all said the same thing: "I thought somebody else had read it." Seven sets of eyes and no one was looking. More inspection does not equal better quality. In fact it has the opposite effect. It reduces quality and drives up cost.

Instead of inspecting, we need to be preventing. This is a hard battle to fight in government because inspections and CYA are kind of our *modus operandi*. How do most laws get created? A one-in-a-million chance happens; a tragedy occurs and elected officials, spurred on by the media, vow to never let it happen again. They create a new agency to oversee and inspect whatever odd thing happened. Then of course, despite all the oversight and inspecting, the odd thing happens again and an investigation is launched and steps are added to inspect the inspectors to make sure this thing never happens again. And on and on it goes. Every screw-up earns more layers of CYA. More eyes looking at it, more sign-offs. When I work with organizations and see these cumbersome CYA-laden processes, I can quickly tell they've had a long history of high-profile mistakes. Rather than figuring out how to prevent mistakes, however, the effort goes toward catching the mistakes.

When our processes are long and filled with handoffs, accountability decreases. When fifteen hands touch it, who is accountable? When our processes are short and handoffs are few, accountability increases. When employees get instant feedback on mistakes and are required to correct their own mistakes, errors drop quickly. When errors are discovered months later and fixed by an error-correction department, nothing gets better.

Cost-saving strategy #3: Do it right the first time.

Cost Driver #4: Specialization. We talked about this extensively in the Fable of Complexity, but it deserves a little more scrutiny in terms of what it does to costs. The first impact specialization has on cost is the obvious one: A Plan Review Specialist III costs more than a Plan Review Specialist II, who costs more than a Plan Reviewer. Higher specialization leads to higher wages and higher costs. Beyond the obvious, though, are the real cost drivers: Specialization creates CYA. Every time we specialize, we create a handoff. You do this, she does that. As we discussed before, every handoff will eventually lead to CYA. At every handoff, we eventually have to log work that comes in, assign it, track it, expedite it, log it out, and transport it. None of that stuff adds value. It just adds cost.

The secret to getting tax refunds out 80 percent faster at less cost was to get rid of handoffs. What took three minutes of actual work was taking three months. The three minutes had been chopped up across fourteen handoffs. Each handoff was a specialist, and between each one there was batching, tracking, logging, and transporting. The team's solution was to eliminate the specialties and in turn eliminate the handoffs. Employees completed the whole tax return from beginning to end in three minutes (the Principle of One at its best).

Specialization creates bottlenecks. The capacity doesn't match the demand, and work piles up. Most bottlenecks are specialists. We wait weeks for legal to sign off on the contract. We wait a month for the council to approve our change. The Specialist III is on vacation and is the only one who can sign off on the review. The more specialization we have, the more chances we are creating for a mismatch between demand and capacity. If your process has five places where only "that guy" can do "that thing," your progress is totally dependent on the availability of those five guys at exactly the right time. (This is why your house doesn't get built in seven days.) Chances are, customers will get stuck and start banging on the pipes.

The effects of specialization are even greater when government creates new programs. Rather than adapting an existing program and its pipes to serve a different population, elected officials create a brand new program and subsequent pipes. If we have a program to fight obesity, we create a totally new program to fight childhood obesity and then another to fight adolescent obesity and still another to address obesity among immigrants. Each program has its own funding stream and its own intake process, application form, and case-management process. All of these pipes then have to be coordinated with the like pipes of all the other programs serving similar populations. It would be akin to Ford creating a new car company every time it created a new car model. What a waste! Instead, Ford utilizes the same factories, distributors, and dealerships to make many models.

Cost-saving strategy #4: Have as few hands touch it as possible.

Cost Driver #5: Management. Perhaps nothing drives up cost as much as the good intentions of management. Take a look at your day. What are you doing today? How much of it is mission work? How much of it moves the water through the pipes? If you're like my workshop participants, you are spending less than 50 percent of your day making the widgets. Where does the other half go? Management. Staff meetings, budget exercises, team-building, accountability sessions, performance reviews, and on an on.

Most of us are working longer hours and feeling like we are accomplishing less. Why? Management. Mold. CYA. They all conspire to rob us of capacity and drive up cost. We spend so much of our time tracking work, controlling work, giving feedback, and holding people accountable that we can't actually get any work done.

I was enduring an especially long trip at a Sam's Club to appease my wife's need for a sixty-pound box of granola, when I walked past the manager's office. On her wall was a giant poster with the phrase,

"Anything you are doing that does not benefit the customer is a complete waste of your time." I almost dropped my sixteen-quart jug of toothpaste right there on the spot. What an amazingly simple way to say what I've been trying to say for fifteen years! Anything you are doing that doesn't benefit the customer is a complete waste of your time. The tracking sheet, the staff meeting, the new initiative kickoff, the hours spent on the dress code policy, the performance appraisals, personal development plans, and the budgeting for results. All of it adds time and cost and reduces capacity. None of it helps the customer.

With anything you or your organization are about to embark on, put it to the Sam's Club test. Or apply it to our pipes metaphor: "Will this action help us move the water more quickly or will it slow us down?" If it slows you down — if it steals capacity — then don't do it. We can't afford it right now. We can come back to it later when the water has receded and the pipes aren't about to burst.

Cost-saving strategy #5: Leave people alone and let them do their work.

When we talk about "Better Faster Cheaper," it's not a best-two-out-of-three situation. You've got to have all three. And you can. But you have to know where to start.

If you start with "cheaper" — that is, with a focus on cutting costs within the systems you already have — you will likely become slower and make more mistakes. Most cost-cutting initiatives — consolidation, furloughs, layoffs, reduced equipment — rob us of capacity. Their effects are compounded when they impact our bottlenecks. Lost capacity slows us down. When things are moving slowly, corners get cut and people rush in order to expedite. These activities drive up mistakes.

If you start with "better" — focusing on quality and on not making mistakes — you will likely become slower and more expensive. When the goal is simply to eradicate mistakes, we often add layers of CYA and additional inspectors. These drive up cost and slow things down.

But if you start with "faster," as I talked about in Chapter 6, you'll actually get the other two. If we speed up the system and unkink the pipes, we can get more done with limited resources. When we go faster, we eliminate the biggest cost-drivers. By going faster, we also increase quality. You can't be fast and make mistakes — you'll get bogged down in rework. To be fast we have to *poka yoke*. To be fast, we must eliminate handoffs and CYA and all the things in the system that cause mistakes. By making the system faster, you increase the capacity of the staff, which allows them to spend more time doing quality work.

Better, faster, cheaper. Start with faster and you get all three.

CHAPTER 9

All Pipes Are Not Created Equal

I was sitting in on a senior staff meeting of an organization the other day (the greatest benefit of my job is not having these myself), and I saw something that left me completely speechless. I really shouldn't have been so surprised, as this was something I had seen countless times in virtually every agency I have visited. Sitting around the table was the director, the deputy director, the general counsel, the chief information officer, the director of administration, the director of human resources, the budget director, and the head of organizational training and development. Arriving late were the two heads of the divisions that actually did the work of the agency's mission. (I was to learn later that these two were the "problem children" who were never "on board.") The eight "leaders" around the table droned on for ninety minutes, stopping for only a few moments to let the operating divisions to put in their two cents.

What was wrong with this meeting — besides the enormous waste of time and money? It was totally upside down.

Senior staff meetings are where the big decisions get made: the budget, policies, procedures, legal positions, training initiatives, technology priorities, and so forth. And many of the decisions are decided on by a vote. As in, "Who here thinks we should pay for the employee recognition program out of Jim's operating budget?" Ten people around the table; two do the mission-driven work. And it's a majority vote. The operating divisions get outvoted every time.

The two divisions that do the actual work of the agency end up serving the other eight, the ones who *should* be supporting *them*. Again, this is upside down.

Let's bring it back to pipes. Every organization has two sets: the big ones that deliver value to the customers so the agency can achieve its mission, and the smaller ones that feed and support the bigger ones.

The mission pipes are the ones that deliver the value. The non-mission pipes exist to support the mission pipe. They feed it people, technology, money, and decisions. They create the legal, physical, and emotional environment in which the work takes place. Without the support systems, the mission systems would struggle to do the work. Without the mission systems, there is no point in having the support pipes. If you don't know which kind of pipe you work in, ask yourself this: "If my process didn't exist, what else would go away?" If the answer is "nothing," you're not the mission. If the answer is "everything," congratulations! You are the mission.

Another simple way to understand this concept is to think in terms of customers. We have great debates in government about who the customer is (an argument I hopefully ended in *We Don't Make Widgets*). One of the simplistic definitions is to view customers as internal or external. External customers exist outside the agency's walls. They're the citizens, businesses, taxpayers, job-seekers, and contractors. Internal customers reside within agency walls. In theory, HR serves managers and employees. In theory, IT serves business-process owners. In theory, legal serves management. But in practice, again, it's all turned upside down.

Mission and support. Which do you suppose should get the top priority?

Everything in this book is geared to the mission pipes. For each key mission pipe you should:

- expose the pipe
- analyze the pipe's performance
- *poka yoke* the entry into the pipe
- triage the flow
- process simultaneously when possible
- eliminate CYA by reducing handoffs
- cut batches
- break bottlenecks
- eliminate backlog
- get off the crazy cycle
- eliminate phone calls.

Do those things, and you will radically improve your agency. You can absorb up to 50 percent more work, 80 percent faster with improved quality. You will have dramatically increased your capacity to do more good. Unfortunately, the capacity of most mission pipes get drained, rather than fed, by the support pipes.

CIOs could help the mission pipes by:

- learning their processes
- seeing where technology is limiting performance
- helping improve the process
- finding the solutions that best fit the new process design.

But instead, CIOs encumber the mission pipes with extra work. They burden the pipes with:

- CYA security policies
- "consolidation" efforts that save the CIO money but rob the mission pipes of flexibility and control

- standards and cross-compatibility efforts that tie performance of the main pipe to the design of all pipes
- excessively long IT procurement processes
- an IT monopoly for support with first-come, first-served help, placing critical mission needs in a queue behind the needs of HR, admin, and so on.

It is the job of the CIO to ensure the IT systems in the mission pipes are:
- available 100 percent of the time
- configured to meet the mission goals
- repaired immediately
- receive top priority for modifications and enhancements.

The CIO should be working proactively to optimize the mission pipes.

Or take human resources. HR should be helping the mission by:
- understanding the skills and abilities needed by mission workforce
- developing customized training to support mission workers
- developing strategies to retain key mission talent
- actively recruiting future mission workers.

Instead, HR burdens the mission pipe by:
- taking too long to fill vacancies
- allowing the 4 percent of bad apples to stay on
- creating uniform HR policies
- pay and classification schemes
- crushing morale with pay-for-performance, performance appraisals, and 360-degree reviews
- mandatory, one-size-fits-all training on supervisory skills, customer service, Throwing Fish, Whale Done, and so on.

It is the job of HR to ensure the employees in the mission pipes are:

- skilled
- productive
- happy
- hired quickly
- removed quickly when necessary.

HR should proactively be serving the mission pipes by:

- understanding the workforce needs for today and the future
- continuously recruiting talent
- customizing training and on-the-job development opportunities
- modifying HR policies that constrain mission pipe performance
- deferring to mission pipe managers on decisions about hiring, firing, disciplinary support, and training needs.

But wait! Aren't we supposed to treat everyone equally?

If the goal of our agency is that everyone be equally miserable, yes. If the goal of our agency is use ever-shrinking resources to accomplish all the good we can in this world, then no.

The reality is this: Your agency's ability to do good work is dependent on a few key systems. The ability of those systems to achieve their purposes is dependent on removing a few key kinks in the pipes. Within those pipes are a few key job classifications that absolutely must always be kept filled with happy and productive people.

This is one of the areas where strategic planning has severely let us down in government. There has been no real strategy. Every agency, program, and division has developed a strategic plan. But true strategy should not be all-inclusive. It should be *exclusive*. Strategy is about identifying the vital few. Strategy says, "This is what's important. This is what's vital. This is what has to get better." It's a handful, not a plateful.

This has proven extraordinarily difficult for HR departments in all sectors, not just government. HR agencies have one of those classic dual roles that impede their ability to do either role well. HR has both a compliance mission and a service mission. Good cop, bad cop. A mission pipe manager's desire to hang on to a key employee by boosting pay is met with uniform salary rules and classification policies and a suggestion to reclassify the employee. A mission pipe manager's desire to recruit a specific person is met with hiring policies, merit system requirements, and candidate lists. Again, I'm not blaming the people in HR. They're thoughtful and skilled, and their hearts are in the right place. But they're unfortunately saddled with this Jekyll and Hyde mission. I'm not suggesting they abandon either role. Instead, HR leaders need to be rabidly cognizant of the dual role and be overly sympathetic to the mission pipe leaders. They need to fulfill their compliance role with as little damage as possible to mission pipe performance — and then bend over backward to provide such extraordinarily good service to mission employees that the compliance stuff is tolerated as the small cost of doing business with such great service.

Perhaps an example will help. I was working with a large state agency on its hiring process. It typically took four or five months to fill a vacancy. The HR department was totally hamstrung by merit rules and state personnel policies. Filling a vacancy required submitting a request, reviewing the classification, ensuring there was money authorized, posting the job, creating a merit candidate list, interviewing potential candidates, and then making an offer. It was exceptionally reactive and geared 100 percent toward fairness compliance rather than service. But my team's data revealed that 80 percent of the hiring was being done in 20 percent of the job classifications. Furthermore, these 20 percent were in the heart of the mission pipe. When these jobs were vacant, production suffered. Mission managers were stuck with a four-month hiring process, a four-week on-boarding process and more weeks of training. Every vacancy not only killed productivity of the mission pipe, it also sucked capacity from mission management. Additionally, during the five-month vacancies, other employees had to pick up the slack, adding more stress for the same pay. This led to more vacancies, and before long these units were in HR hell.

How did the team solve this productivity cyclone? Perpetual hiring. For the 20 percent of jobs that caused 80 percent of the work, they created an entirely new, proactive hiring process. HR perpetually recruited, interviewed, and cleared prospective employees. Then, when an employee quit, the mission manager simply placed a call to HR and had a suitable replacement in the chair before it ever got cold.

The same principles apply to legal, budget, and facilities functions — and even the mailroom. Those pipes exist to serve the mission pipes. That service should be impeccable. At the least, those pipes shouldn't rob the mission pipes of capacity. At best, they should do everything possible to proactively increase the mission pipes' capacity to do more good. Support pipes are successful when the mission pipes are successful.

Label Your Pipes

Go underground in any large building, and you'll see a rainbow of color-coded pipes, a different hue for hot water, sewage, the gas line, and so on. The pipes are marked in bold colors so that it's easy for repairmen to see where problems are.

Government agencies need to do the same thing. Your mission pipes and your support pipes should be clearly marked so there is no confusion.

Here are some practical tips for changing the support culture:

1. Staff meetings. Operations divisions — the mission pipes — speak first. Support functions go last. Further, the operating divisions get to function like the U.S. at the United Nations Security Council: They can veto any measure being proposed.

2. Planning. Operating divisions complete their strategic and operating plans first. All other plans are about how to help the operating divisions meet their goals. The performance measure for every support function is whether the mission systems met their goals. They are only successful if the mission pipes are successful.

3. Form teams to improve the support pipes that have the biggest impact on the mission pipes, such as hiring, procurement, IT support functions. At least half of the team should be composed of mission managers and employees, the "customers" of these support pipes.

4. Mission pipe requests get first priority in all organization-wide queues. That includes things like budget needs, IT system enhancements, workforce planning, facility improvements, reclassifications, and legislative agenda items.

5. Give mission pipe members special hats, better coffee, and their own secret handshake. (Just kidding.)

With privilege comes responsibility. The mission managers only receive this special attention because of how vital their operations are. And because their operations are so vital, they have a moral and organizational obligation to be the best in the world at what they do. If they're policing streets, then they need to continuously seek ways to be the best in the world at it. If they're investigating child abuse, then they have a moral responsibility to be the best in the world at it.

It's a simple deal: Mission pipes get first priority in IT, budget, legal, and HR. They have direct access to the top executive in charge.

In return, mission pipe managers must strive to be the best in the world. They should:

1. Continuously improve processes, finding ways to get way more done at less cost and at higher quality.
2. Use data to make decisions and communicate results to the top executive and other shareholders.
3. Interact with customers to identify what they want and what they're getting, and close that gap.
4. Develop the workforce.
5. Use long-range and short-term planning to set clear priorities and get things done.
6. Innovate.
7. Achieve results.

It's a fair trade.

CHAPTER 10

Technology

Instead of raising your hand to ask a question in class, how about individual push buttons on each desk? That way, when you want to ask a question, you just push the button and it lights up a corresponding number on a tote board at the front of the class. Then all the professor has to do is check the lighted number against a master sheet of names and numbers to see who is asking the question.

— from "Deep Thoughts" by Jack Handey

When people are confronted with the hard work of straightening pipes, one of the first reactions I always hear is, "Thank goodness we don't have to worry about doing that. *We're* getting a new technology system."

There are two phrases that will fundamentally destroy the productivity of your agency. The first, as we chronicled in Chapter 5, is, "Never let it happen again." The second is, "We are getting a new system."

The moment you utter, "We are getting a new system," all improvements halt for ten years. Think about it. From the moment you decide you want a new tech system until you've gotten approval, created a requirements document and run the RFP gauntlet — how long does that take? For most public-sector agencies, it's about two years. During that two-year period, you can forget trying to implement any changes to your current process. Think about the reaction: "Why are you worried about the old process? We are getting a new system. Improving the current process would be wasteful." Two years; zero improvement.

From the moment you select a vendor and bring them on board, until the moment they're finished analyzing, coding, and building the new system — how long does that take? Let's say the vendor tells you two years, meaning you can double it to four. (I'm convinced that most IT vendors were home builders in a previous life.) During that four-year period, you may have all kinds of great ideas about improving the current process. But again, the reaction will be, "Are you nuts? Why are you worried about the old process? The new system goes live in three months!" (And then three more months, then three more months. ...) Six years; zero improvement.

Finally the vendor has the system coded and is ready to flip the switch. Unfortunately, the system's not totally stable yet. If you breathe on it or you look at it wrong, it completely collapses. "And you want to change something? Are you nuts?" Six years and six months; zero improvement.

Now we're almost seven years into our miracle cure, and nothing has gotten any better. Eventually, the system actually gets up and running and starts spitting out widgets. (Or it doesn't: The horrifying reality is that fewer than half of these projects actually make it to the finish line. Imagine what your neighborhood would look like if half the houses were abandoned before they were finished.) In the meantime, you've been sitting on process-improvement ideas for seven years. Now you want to share them. What will the reaction be? "Are you nuts? We finally got this stupid thing working, and now you want to change it?" You will also hear a rousing chorus of, "Get in line," and, "Wait for Version 2.0."

In place of any actual improvement, you get ten years of lost productivity, headaches, contract negotiations, legal battles, embarrassing mistakes, and the loss of your best people to the project team. For what? A 50 percent chance that your hard work and $100 million will pay off. It's a $100 million coin flip.

So why in the heck does anybody do it?

There's no quicker way to appear to be a leader — while simultaneously abdicating your leadership duties — than to announce plans for a new tech system. On one hand, you look "leaderly" by listening to the organization's problems, searching the world for a solution, and then marshaling the support to allocate bucket loads of scarce resources to buy something futuristic and sexy. But on the other hand, all improvements cease for a decade, and you're handing your fate over to private-sector vendors who don't understand your agency and don't report to you. As a leader, you're basically saying, "I have found the cure for the common cold. It's going to make us terribly sick and there is only a 50 percent chance it will work. Oh, and by the way, the cure will take so long that I won't be around to see if you live or die. Good luck." Pity the poor leader who comes along next, who must testify before an angry budget committee as to where all the money went and why the "cure" had to be abandoned.

Having said all that, that's not the real reason why technology is not the answer. Technology is not the answer because technology is not the problem.

Technology is not the reason we have seven sign-offs on every document. It's not why we have bottlenecks holding up the flow, or the reason we have a nine-month backlog and an ever-expanding call center. Technology is not the reason we've chopped up work into a million small pieces and then built a hierarchy to control them all.

These aren't technology problems. These are system problems. These problems are cultural and managerial — not technical. They are issues of work design, values, and trust — not servers, platforms, and interfaces.

Despite their bold, disease-curing claims, people in the IT community know this better than anyone. We bring them our rusty, twisted, kinked-up pipes and ask them to automate them. They reply, "Are you going to do anything about the fact that seven people have to sign off on these documents?" No, we say. Just automate the whole process. "What about that bottleneck over there or the huge pile of backlog? Will you be doing anything about that?" Nah, just automate it.

We don't do anything to actually fix the system; we just want a totally new one. So the IT providers give us back a new set of pipes that look remarkably like the old pipes, only shinier. They have the same twists, the same kinks, and the same inability to handle all the water.

What the IT vendor has essentially done is what's referred to as "paving cowpaths." If you look at aerial photos of most county road systems, their pathways defy logic. That's because logic wasn't the design concept. Many county roads owe their origin to the paths farmers used to take their cows to market. Over time, these well-worn paths became established trails. Eventually, when it was time to put down paved roads, these twisted, seemingly aimless journeys got a nice coat of asphalt. We are now stuck with them, and we re-pave their inefficiency every ten to fifteen years. Sound familiar?

The other reason technology is not the answer goes back to our discussion of elapsed time versus work time. You will remember that work time is the amount of time in a process where work actually occurs. Elapsed time is the total amount of time consumed by the process. It is what the customer experiences. You will also recall that the work time is typically less than 5 percent of the elapsed time. Yet of those two, which is technology most likely to address? Work time. That is what technology does: It makes our work tasks easier to perform. What used to take two ledgers and an abacus can now be done on one screen. What used to involve getting files from here and there can now be done at the click of a button. Technology makes tasks easier. But the tasks are only 5 percent of the issue. We invest $40 million — or

$60 million, or $100 million — to improve 5 percent of the problem!

And where do you suppose most of that $100 million has been spent? Automating payroll, HR, finance, fleet, and budget. Non-mission pipes! We have been robbing the resources of the mission pipes — the value-creating pipes — in order to automate the support pipes. And what do the mission pipes get in return? Their people, money, technology, and facilities are now delivered on freshly paved, inflexible cowpaths. Again, it's all upside down. Technology investments should be made to improve the capacity of the mission pipes, not detract.

Let me be clear, I'm not a Luddite. I wrote this book on an iPad (so if you don't like it, take it back to the Apple store and get a refund). My windshield has so many gadgets on it that I have to lean out the window, golden retriever-style, to see where I'm going. Technology definitely has a role to play in transforming our systems, just not at the beginning.

Technology is our friend when it enables us to straighten the pipes by, for example, greatly reducing task time for a bottleneck resource or allowing us to route work in a parallel versus sequential fashion. Technology also can help us *poka yoke* a process. Data-entry screens that don't allow customers to enter incorrect information are one example. Or real-time edits that ding at employees when they've entered a likely-incorrect value. And technology can be used to help improve the customer experience. Online car registration renewals, for instance, have allowed millions of people to take care of their needs over the Web, clearing out DMV lobbies nationwide.

When technology eliminates transactions, errors, phone calls, and wait times — the actual drivers of cost and waste in government — then it is our ally. When it increases CYA, specialization, handoffs, backlogs, batches, and bottlenecks, it is our enemy. When technology seeks to pave old cowpaths, we must stand in front of the bulldozers. But when it allows us to blaze new trails, let's climb aboard.

Old School

Your view of technology and my argument are probably going to be generational. For those of us who grew up looking at a pale green cursor flash numbly on a dumb terminal — or who have ever seen an overdue report suddenly disappear and get replaced by the Blue Screen of Death — the virtues of technology have to be taken a bit on faith. For those who learned their ABCs on a smartphone app, the view is quite different. The benevolence of technology is a given. Steve Jobs exists, and he answers prayers directly.

I was reminded of this when I was working with a county government in a high-tech corridor. The employees were all young, hip, and tech-savvy. We were discussing an old procurement process I had worked on, and I happened to mention the color goldenrod. They stared at me as if I was speaking in tongues. I asked them, "Surely you've heard of goldenrod? And salmon and magenta?" Nothing. For anybody over age 30, we remember these colors vividly. Most government forms were always copied in triplicate. There was the original, the goldenrod copy, the magenta copy, and the salmon copy. The young employees laughed at me. "That is so old school! We don't have any copies. We have a state-of-the-art procurement system. Everything is electronic!"

I'm not in the habit of betting my audiences, but I couldn't resist. "Over lunch, I want you to get some data about the procurement process. Let's see how long the process took before the automation and how long it takes now." They returned from lunch dumbfounded. Procurement took longer now than it ever had before. How could that be?

Well, they had a new system and the system allowed them to do electronic approvals. This greatly reduced paper, and it cut transportation time between approvers. Unfortunately, their culture of CYA dictated that these approvals be sequential. That is, when Joe logged in and approved a requisition, an electronic message was sent to Mary alerting her that she could make her approval when she was ready. And on down the line. ...

The whole point of goldenrod, magenta, and salmon was to accommodate simultaneous processing. All three forms could be routed to the appropriate person for simultaneous approval. We got made fun of in government for filling out forms in triplicate, but what appeared to be inefficient from a task perspective was actually quite efficient from a system perspective. Couldn't their fancy new system have been programmed to do this same thing? Yep. But remember, their problems were not technical. They were cultural, managerial, and trust issues.

CHAPTER 11

The Transformation

"Your best thinking got you here."
— *Alcoholics Anonymous*

It's time to make over our house. We need to tear out the pipes, knock down the walls, and eradicate the mold. We need more capacity so that we can do more good. We need nothing short of a transformation. Unlike on TV, our transformation likely won't be done in seven days. But it will follow a predictable path. All transformations — organizational or personal — go through the same three stages: Get it, do it, live it.

Get It

Last fall, a friend of mine had on one of those rubber cause bracelets — this one was purple. I knew what most of the colors stood for, but I hadn't encountered a purple one before. So I asked what it was for. He said, "It's a reminder to stop complaining. Every time I complain, I move it to the other wrist. The goal is to keep it on the same wrist for twenty-one straight days. After that, I should be able to live pretty much complaint-free."

Now, I'd known this guy for over a decade. He had elevated complaining from a pastime to a hobby to a serious craft. So I laughed it off and said, "Good luck! You're going to need it."

Twenty-one days without complaining? I couldn't go twenty-one seconds. And why would you want to? What would there be to talk about? I just didn't get it.

And that's when I got it.

In complaining about not complaining, I sounded like all the people in my workshops who, even when they're confronted with a new idea or a big change, still don't do it. They don't get it. And if they don't get it, they certainly won't do it, much less live it.

To paraphrase Einstein, the significant problems we face cannot be solved at the same level of thinking that created them. Both Einstein and my bracelet-wearing friend had the same point: We need to elevate our consciousness. That is, before any transformation is possible, we must engage the mind in a new perspective. This can be as simple as reading a book or hearing someone talk on TV or listening to a friend. Sometimes it comes to us out of nowhere — a book falls off a shelf and hits us in the foot; we wake up in the morning with an *aha!* or we see a friend we haven't run into for years and they seem so different. Whatever it is, something happens that expands our awareness. This is why conferences can be so powerful. This is why I encourage people to read my book and pass it on. It slips the concepts into the consciousness. And to quote Anne Hathaway (Shakespeare's wife, not the actress), "A mind once expanded can never return to its original dimensions." When something enters our awareness, we then make a choice: Is this for me or not? We don't "get it" at that stage, we just make the decision whether to investigate further.

Once a new concept is in our consciousness, we then follow a strange mix of fact and emotion before we truly "get it." The mind first goes through a logical progression starting with:

Believing we have a problem. Anyone familiar with twelve-step programs knows this is the first step. Anyone who's ever worked in sales also knows that if you don't get past this step, nothing else you say matters. No matter how glorious the idea, solution, or program may look, I'm not going to do it if I don't think I need to. This is exactly where I was with complaining. Sure I complained, but who didn't? But that's the funny thing about our consciousness: Once an idea gets in, it tends to show up over and over again until we deal with it. The more I told myself that complaining wasn't a big deal, the more aware I became of how much I complained. But it wasn't until I asked other people about my complaining that I realized I truly had a problem. This is the premise behind interventions: We often don't accept that we have a problem until confronted with the impact our behavior has on other people. This is doubly true for organizations. We may think our organization is customer-focused until we actually go ask our customers. We may think we value our employees until we spend time with them and find out we've got a problem. I'm often asked in my workshops how to get "the people upstairs to get it." My answer is always that they should spend time with customers and employees. Stage an organizational intervention. When we accept that we may have a problem, the next step is:

Believing the solution will work. Just because we admit that we need to change doesn't mean we will embrace the solution being presented. Wearing a bracelet will help me stop complaining? How is a purple bracelet going to make the lady at the checkout counter move any faster? How is a purple bracelet going to get my lost luggage back? Our minds start fact-finding, usually to refute the new idea. Again, this is a strange mix of facts and emotions. We'll read the claims — that less complaints mean lower stress, say, or that process improvement in your agency will help you do more with limited resources — but we don't totally believe the claims until we see the results with our own eyes. For organizational transformation, one of the most powerful ways to do this is to get in the van and go visit an agency that has been through the transformation. Hanging out with someone who never complains is actually quite inspiring. Visiting an agency that is truly living a mission of service to customers and employees is equally inspiring. After this fact-finding, unless we are in total denial, we accept the solution is possible and then make a critical calculation:

Believing the benefits are worth the effort. All change requires discomfort and effort, neither of which we'll endure if we don't think we have a problem or don't truly desire the benefits. When big effort is required for a small benefit, we put up resistance. When the benefits are small and distant, and the effort is large and immediate, it's easier not to even try.

Even after all this factual wrestling with a new awareness, we still must come to believe that change is the right thing for us. Once we truly know we "need" change, we're ready. So what exactly do we have to "get" in order to transform our house? I've asked you to "get" a lot of ideas in this book:

- That government is not different — all work is a system, regardless of industry or profession.
- That to improve an organization you have to improve the systems of the organization.
- That the systems — our pipes — are where all the action is. Our results come from our pipes. Our customers show up in our pipes. Our employees work in the pipes. Our costs are all in the pipes.
- That we have but one problem in government — capacity. Our pipes can't keep up with the flood of water coming in.
- That the secret to increasing capacity is to go faster. The faster the water can move through our pipes, the more water we can handle.
- That we go faster by straightening our pipes, removing the fifteen years of CYA, the handoffs, the batches, backlogs, and bottlenecks. By doing these things, we can go 80 percent faster, greatly increasing our capacity to do more good.

- That we can go faster without compromising quality. We don't cut corners or rush; instead, we eliminate the lost time in the system, allowing each customer to flow through our pipes quickly and allowing workers to have the time required to do a great job.
- That costs are in the system. Rather than outsiders cutting expenses, we need insiders cutting costs. When we straighten the pipes, we eliminate the true sources of costs: time, transactions, mistakes, and management.

In essence, what we need to get is systems thinking. To see problems as systems problems. To see that the opportunities are in our systems.

The other notion I've asked you to get is that all the other stuff that's not focused on improving systems actually makes things worse. Focusing on people, holding them accountable and trying to motivate them just spreads mold and makes everyone sick. I've been pretty critical of a lot of "best practices" — pay-for-performance, results-oriented management, strategic planning, stretch targets, consolidations, privatization, suggestion systems, blue ribbon commissions, and technology. I don't do this just to be a contrarian. Rather, by laying waste to all the other approaches, I'm hoping to tear down your defenses. I'm burning all the ships so you have no choice but to stay on the island and focus on the only thing that works: fixing systems. As the twelve-step programs know, people usually won't accept treatment until they have exhausted all other means. Alcoholics Anonymous has a great slogan: "Your best thinking got you here." In other words, by trying to do things "your way," look at what a mess you've made.

The same is true for us. Our best thinking has gotten us where we are today, and it ain't pretty. By being critical of that best thinking, I've tried to accelerate our hitting rock bottom so that we'll stop flailing and instead reach for the one thing that can save us: systems thinking. These other approaches don't fix systems. Many of them make systems worse. The moldy approaches perpetuate a fear-based culture. They see people and organizations through a distorted lens. As I mentioned in Chapter 3, changing the thinking won't be enough. We need a heart transplant. We need a holistic healing.

Guerrilla Warfare

How do you create change when you're not in charge? What if you "get it" but the leadership doesn't? When top management isn't supportive of a change initiative, you have only one recourse left: Go underground. Here's how.

1. Find a supportive manager. Guerrilla warfare starts with two people: a brave change agent and an enlightened manager. No matter how backward your organization may be, there is at least one manager who "gets it," who wants to make her unit the best it can be. Find this person and indoctrinate her. Attend a seminar or conference together. Take her to lunch, or give her an article. Just do something to pique her interest. Discuss how the proposed change initiative (its concepts and methods) will impact the things she cares about. Often, this enlightened manager will be you. In that case, you play both roles. Be the change agent you want to see elsewhere.

2. Implement the change initiative in one unit. Once you have found your comrade-in-arms, it's time to get to work. Together, draft a game plan for how to implement the change initiative in her unit. Involve others she trusts in the discussion. Start with one project and one team. Focus on areas that will have high impact and a high probability of success. Make dramatic improvements that force everyone — customers inside the organization and out, employees, upper management — to take notice. The response you want is, "How did you do that?"

What will it take for government to finally get these concepts? To really "do it" and "live it"? Government needs proof. We need people to show the way. If we have enough enlightened leaders transforming their agencies using these principles, others will follow. Nobody believed

Don't make the mistake of piloting the concepts on low-hanging fruit. Think big. We're not talking about moving the coffee-maker closer to the break room. If nobody notices what you've done, you've missed the point of guerrilla warfare. And if everybody notices what you are doing before you're done, you have also missed the point.

3. Create a buzz. Ideally, the results of the project will be evident to everyone. You want to hear conversations at the water cooler that start with, "Did you hear what they pulled off in Mary's unit?" There are other strategies for creating buzz, too. Celebrate employees' accomplishments wildly, in a way that makes every take notice and become interested. You can also obtain external recognition for accomplishments. Maybe your higher-ups aren't interested, but professional organizations and other outside groups certainly will be.

You don't have to be in charge or have full control to make great change. Stop waiting for the new computer system or executive enlightenment. They aren't coming. Change can begin with you, wherever you are. Good luck on your guerrilla mission, and remember the old maxim: "It is easier to beg forgiveness than to ask permission."

you could build a house in seven days until they saw it on TV. Nobody will believe you can work 80 percent faster — with better quality and lower costs, while having a fully engaged workforce — until they see it. If you "get it," help others get it too.

Do It

There's a 600-year-old Chinese saying: "To know and not to do is not to know." We can know something conceptually, but only when we've actually experienced something are we truly able to get it. I read every book imaginable about parenting, but it wasn't until my young son lay in a hospital bed with a broken arm and face full of terror that I truly "got it." It is important to understand, personally and organizationally, that you don't have to truly "buy in" all the way before you "do it." In fact, real transformation often involves bouncing back and forth between getting it and doing it. We think we have something figured out, we do it, we fail, and we go learn some more. The constant interplay between getting it and doing it is what leads to mastery. Unfortunately, organizationally and personally, we often try something, fail, and then immediately conclude that it doesn't work, or that we can't do it. Then we move on to something else. We try thirty different diets. We try the patch, the gum, a bracelet, and a support group to stop smoking. We keep searching for the one that will work.

But the key is to go deeper. If you're searching for water, it's better to dig one well a hundred feet deep than to dig a hundred wells a foot deep. Any approach followed with discipline can lead to transformation. Any approach that's dabbled in, sort-of understood, and haphazardly applied can lead to failure, wasted effort, and cynicism. Commit to change: Embrace it, practice it, and master it.

Back to my experience with the purple "no complaints" bracelet: Once I understood that I *needed* a complaint-free life, I actually slipped one of the purple bracelets on my right wrist. Again, the goal was to go twenty-one days without complaining. Each time I complained, I was supposed to switch the bracelet to my other wrist. By mid-morning I had nearly broken my bracelet. After lunch with a waitress who had still not realized her full potential (see how this no-complaining stuff makes a difference?), I had to get a new bracelet. I was dumbfounded by how often I complained and how hard it was going to be to stop. My first inclination was to quit: My goal just didn't seem possible. We do this all the time in our organizations. We try, we fail, and we quit.

How do we break this pattern? We need a finger. When infants first start walking, they inevitably will take a couple wobbly steps and then collapse. Parents don't say, "Well, this walking thing isn't going to work. Guess you're stuck crawling." No, parents give their children a hand to hold on to, then two fingers, then one, and eventually we let go. With any new thing we're trying in our organizations, we should reach for a finger to grasp — a trusted adviser or an agency that has already been through a similar change. If you can't find that finger, create one. Start a support group. Like walking, the early stages of transformation are about stumbling and learning. Rather than glossing over those early struggles, we should use them as a chance to discuss and learn. To fail and not learn anything is to fail twice.

The other thing that derails transformation is the often slow pace of results. We expend the effort up front, but the payback can be months away. It's hard to keep eating fists full of broccoli when the scale keeps showing the same number. It's hard to keep tracking performance data when nothing seems to be getting better. Our natural desire is to quit. And unless this effort is truly addressing a need, as opposed to a want, we probably will.

How long does transformation take? Think about this. According to Will Bowen, the creator of the complaint-free bracelets and the Complaint Free World Program, it takes twenty-one days to form a new habit. By going twenty-one consecutive days without complaining, we have broken ourselves of the habit of complaining and replaced it with a new habit of gratitude and a positive outlook. We have essentially re-wired our brains. If personal behavior takes twenty-one days to change, how does that translate into organizational behavior? Most organizational change efforts happen in projects. Each project takes three to four months. So a personal day is roughly equivalent to three to four months organizationally. Multiply that by twenty-one and you get a rough idea why true transformation requires discipline.

I remember one organization I worked with where we were roughly two years into a transformation effort to radically improve business processes for customers. Since the transformation's inception, we had held quarterly meetings to go over performance measures. At each meeting my team questioned the numbers, prodded the analysis and begged for action. The managers didn't "get it" and they were only "doing it" because they had to. Then one quarter, a manager got up and showed a chart with some declining numbers. Before we could get the questions out of our mouths, he said, "We formed a team to study the process, and they made six excellent recommendations. And you will see these numbers turn by the end of the year." That's when we turned the corner.

I still remember the first time I went an entire day without complaining. I was flying to the West Coast and both legs of my flight had been delayed significantly. When we finally took off, the air-conditioning on the plane worked about as well as my seatmate's shower apparently had, and the flight attendant brought me the wrong beverage. My normal behavior pattern would have been to complain about all of it and then forecast lost baggage, an overbooked hotel, and whatever other gloom-and-doom scenario my inconvenienced mind could concoct. But the reality was that I was in a chair in the sky being whisked to a place thousands of miles away to work with a wonderful group of people to solve really important problems. I had nothing to complain about. So I didn't. And four months later I actually made it twenty-one straight days without any complaints. (It would have been sooner, but Will Bowen informed me that sarcasm — my second language — is merely complaining with a punch line.)

As we work to transform our agencies, there is a key concept we must "get" before we try to "do." We need to focus. One of my favorite quotes, usually attributed to the Archbishop Oscar Romero, is, "We cannot do everything, and there is a sense of liberation in realizing that. This enables us to do something, and to do it very, very well."

Put another way, it's not important that we do everything well, but that we do the really important things really well. What are those vital few things that, if done extremely well, will fundamentally transform your culture? What are the key pipes? Focus on the mission pipes, the three to five vital systems that deliver your results. Direct your energy toward straightening those few pipes, and you'll achieve radical results in a short period of time.

Unfortunately, we usually go about things in the opposite way. Once we've decided something is important, we think that we can't make progress until everyone has given their "buy-in." That's a mistake. Experience has taught me (which is my way of saying I have no data on this) that whatever it is you are trying to do, about 20 percent of the staff will be with you from the get-go. Another 60 percent will be on the fence, waiting to see if this too shall pass. The final 20 percent aren't coming with you no matter what you say or do. Yet where do we spend all our effort? We invest so much time and energy at the outset trying to convince the 60 percent (who will only believe it when they "see" it, not "hear") and trying to force the last 20 percent, we neglect the 20 percent who were with us from the start. We need to flip this. Spend 80 percent of your time with the 20 percent who want to follow you. Or, to borrow a phrase from the George W. Bush administration, go with the "coalition of the willing." Equip them, support them, and help them complete their mission. Let their success get people off the fence.

Once your crew is in place and you've color-coded your pipes, you can begin the rebuilding process. And here, just like on TV, you can complete the makeover in seven days. Radically improving any process takes about forty hours of hard labor from a team. Typically, those forty hours are broken up into twenty two-hour meetings, stretching the elapsed time to six or nine months. We don't have that kind of time anymore.

The new approach to improvement projects (often called Kaizens or blitzes) works much like *Extreme Makeover*: Lock people in a room on Monday and let them out on Friday. Do the forty hours of work in five days (we have to let them eat and sleep) instead of six months. This focused intensity delivers amazing results.

Here's a step-by-step plan for pulling off one-week makeovers:

Before the show airs:

Be clear about which pipe you're straightening. Embedded in that sentence are two key concepts: that you are fixing a pipe (not working on squishy, abstract things like morale, engagement, or communication), and that you are fixing *one* pipe. Before you get to work, define that pipe clearly. Where does it start? Where does it stop? What comes out of it? Who uses it? What results is it supposed to accomplish? I encourage groups that I work with to draw a picture of it.

Be clear about who owns the pipe. Who has the authority to commission this remodel? Whom are you building the house for? The scope of the project must match the authority of the project. It does little good to embark on a total home renovation only to find out that the person who championed it is the teenager upstairs. We can remodel his bedroom, but if we touch the kitchen, his mom's going to kill us.

Determine who has the authority to approve recommendations to the whole pipe. Then cross your fingers and hope that person "gets it." If he doesn't, and if he can't be convinced, you need to choose a different pipe or a different section where you do have a supportive sponsor.

Put the right people on the crew. Straightening the pipes is best done as a team activity. Rarely does one person have the insight and expertise to redesign the whole thing. Just like a home remodel, you need carpenters, plumbers, roofers, and electricians. Find people inside the system as well as people affected by the system. Make sure your team is the right size. Ideally, that means six to eight people. You need diversity of ideas, but the marginal utility of each person above eight is minimal. Choose people who know the current system but aren't too close to it. Nobody likes having their baby called ugly. Choose people who can play nicely together. The reality show we want is *Extreme Makeover: Home Edition,* not *Real Housewives of New Jersey* or *Big Brother.*

The crew needs a foreman. The foreman doesn't do the work; he or she directs the crew. These people are what I call change agents. They have the knowledge, skills, and tools to help teams create radical improvements. They get things done through their keen ability to facilitate groups of people through well-defined processes to develop and sell new ideas. My first book, *The Change Agent's Guide to Radical Improvement,* is a tools book written especially for these people. Using the tools in the context of our one-week project, foremen can guide their teams to tremendous outcomes.

The week of the show:

Project orientation. The team comes together and hears from the project sponsor just what exactly they've gotten themselves into. Clarify the scope, the roles, and the expectations of the project.

Understand the pipe. To understand the pipe, you have to actually see it. Get out and walk the pipe from beginning to end. This often-overlooked step creates consensus about what truly happens in the pipe (as opposed to what is supposed to happen), and it creates a shared context for what happens next: the map. There are any number of tools that can be used to map a process, some more painful than others. I am partial to IMT Inc.'s FACT sheet tool I mentioned in *The Change Agent's Guide to Radical Improvement.* It clearly shows who is involved in the process and what they are doing, but most importantly it identifies the elapsed time and work time of each step in the process. The team can easily see the size of the opportunity (almost always 95 percent or higher) and zoom in on where all that opportunity is. If any team member didn't "get it" before the project, they certainly will at this stage.

Analyze the pipe. Analyze the pipe from three perspectives: what the data tells you (the volume of water, the elapsed time, the work time, and the capacity of the pipe); what your customers tell you (what they experience and what they *want* to experience); and those things that rob you of capacity (batches, backlog, bottlenecks, CYA, and so forth).

Straighten the pipe. If the problem is a bottleneck, find a way around it. If there's backlog, come up with a plan to get out of it and never get behind again. Where processes are sequential, make them parallel. Where customers are stuck in a one-size-fits-all pipe, create express pipes and triage systems. *Poka yoke* the front of the pipe and all the places where mistakes are commonly made. Come up with a blueprint for the new process. The new pipe should be much shorter and straighter, capable of moving lots more water in a lot less time at less cost.

Sell the idea. Convince your sponsor that the blueprint is good. Make sure the sponsor "gets it" — she believes there's a problem, believes that the solution will work, and believes that the reward will be worth the effort. Be especially certain that you have the real financial decision-maker at the table. Often the person we think runs the house isn't really the one who does.

Implementation. Once the blueprint is approved, the demolition can begin. Just like on the TV show, this is where you'll need a lot more hands. The new process design will likely involve big changes to policies, procedures, job descriptions, training, and even technology. You need all hands on deck to rebuild these things as quickly as possible. Again, you can drag that out as long as you wish or you can treat it like the TV makeover. Unlike my homebuilder, you will want to check back in with the residents after they have moved into their remodeled home. Houses settle, drywall cracks, and the plumber forgets to put seals on the toilets. All new implementations will need some minor modifications and repairs.

Repeat these same six steps for each of your key pipes. Most agencies have three to five key pipes, meaning you can redesign your agency in a few short months. The full transformation will take longer, but the redesign phase can happen quite swiftly. From there you can move into straightening the support pipes, which will add further capacity to the mission pipes.

Live It

The final phase of transformation is actually living it. If we truly get it, we have the discipline to do it — to fail, learn, and do it some more — then living it can be the easy part. Does that mean we won't slip back in to our old ways? We won't sneak a double-cheeseburger or complain that there weren't enough pickles on it? We won't try to close a future budget gap by counting paper clips? Of course we will slip. But when we are living it, we slip less and we get back up faster. I still put the purple bracelet on from time to time to remind me about the importance of not complaining (especially if I'm visiting the in-laws).

You'll know you are living it when you truly can't imagine going back to the old way. A complaint-free life is amazing. Food tastes better (or at least you tell yourself it does), relationships are stronger, and long lines at the checkout counter are a chance to learn why Jen and Angelina will never get along. In fact, if you are looking for a way to truly transform your organization, try making it a complaint-free organization, one that practices gratitude — for its people, its customers, its challenges, and successes. I can think of no better way to live, and no better way to work.

Living it, in the context of this book, means straightening the pipes and eradicating mold. And that means:

- seeing problems as system problems, not people problems. We ask why, not who.
- managing systems, not people. We talk about systems. We measure systems. We plan for systems. We troubleshoot systems.
- improving systems, not people. We put away all of our efforts to change, motivate, and incentivize people. Instead, we use all that energy to put our good people on *Extreme Makeover* crews to radically improve the systems.
- using data to understand systems, not to hold people accountable. We understand variation, knowing when to act and when not to. We understand that if you don't like the results we're getting that yelling, incentivizing, and target-setting won't get us anywhere. When we want better results, we build better systems.
- treating our people like the volunteers that they are. (They don't have to work here, and they don't have to give their discretionary effort.) We continuously engage their hearts and minds to contribute to this grand mission we are a part of. We remove the parts of our workplace that de-motivate our employees and find more and more ways to allow their intrinsic motivation to flourish by giving them chances for mastery, autonomy, and, of course, purpose.

This life is not for everyone. Some in your organization will move through the "get it" and "do it" stage quite quickly. Others will never truly get it. It's important where you spend your energy. We are after hearts and minds here, not compliance. Just like *Extreme Makeover,* we want people on the crew who are doing it because they want to contribute, not because they were told to show up.

Too often, a large organization will see something that's working in one unit and decide to mandate that for every unit. Say one department is using a balanced scorecard because they're "living" the idea of using data to make decisions, and they're achieving great results. Suddenly mandating that every other department adopt balanced scorecards isn't going to work. You can't mandate excellence. You can make people do things, but they will never "live it" because they don't "get it." When we do this — when we try to change others — all the energy comes from us. It's like watching someone try to drag a horse that doesn't want to move. All we can do for someone else is to help them through the three phases. We can help them "get it," we can support them as they try to "do it," and we can be a partner as they "live it." But the decision to change is a personal one, and we can't rush someone through the phases. Some units will "get it" quickly and start doing it. Some units have already been living it a long time and don't need to "get it." And others will "get it" only when they truly need it. A good leader recognizes which phases everyone is in and knows the right thing to do to help them on their journey.

We are after passion, not compliance. We want people's hearts, not their half-hearted efforts.

My favorite part of *Extreme Makeover: Home Edition* is the big reveal. This is the moment that all the work is done, the crowd is assembled. The crew moves a bus out of the way, revealing the new home to the grateful recipients. It is one of the most moving moments on television. The crew is crying, the crowd is crying, and of course the homeowners are bawling their eyes out. All for one reason: gratitude. Gratitude for the new home. Gratitude that the community came together. Gratitude that volunteers were able to contribute their talent and skills to a worthy cause.

Our agencies can have the same moment and the same impact. We can flood the streets with gratitude. Our customers will be grateful because they can get what they need when they need it. Our employees will be grateful because we have engaged their hearts and minds. We have challenged them, and their skills have risen to meet the challenge. And our community will be grateful because they will see a government that works, a government worthy of the sacrifices our forefathers made and the sacrifices our soldiers continue to make. Worthy of the sacrifice good men and women make every day to fund the vital work of government.

The greatest lesson of *Extreme Makeover* is who the crew is building the houses for. These aren't vanity projects. They are gifts to deserving people whose homes have less capacity then their hearts. These are people who make a difference in the world. They are adopting needy children, role-modeling how to live with a crippling disease, or they're the families of those who made the ultimate sacrifice for their nation. They don't just deserve a better home; they need a better home to continue to make this world a better place.

We are no different. We don't just deserve a better organizational home, we need one. We need more capacity to do all the good our citizens need us to do in this world.

The work of government is noble.

The people of government are amazing.

The systems of government are a mess.

When the people in the system — alongside those affected by the system — work together to improve the system, true greatness emerges.

Grab a wrench and join the crew.

Appendix

I have reprinted here one of my most requested articles from Governing.com.

Frustrated by an Unchangeable Agency? Change Anyway.

Sept. 10, 2009

I was concluding a "Better Faster Cheaper" workshop last month with a wonderful set of government managers. These people were bright; they got the concepts; and their hearts were in the right place. But they felt defeated: Tired of fighting to change a seemingly unchangeable system, these folks were worn out.

They peppered me with questions that were all variations on the same theme: "Why bother? Why try?" The only answer that kept coming to me was, "Because it's the right thing to do." I didn't like the answer as it left my mouth each time. It felt like a pat cliché. But as I reflected on it on the flight home, I came to be at peace with it. It was the right answer. It is the only answer.

My answer reminded me of one of those viral emails I received a few years ago, a list of something called the Paradoxical Commandments, or "Anyway." Originally misattributed to Mother Teresa (she had them posted on her wall in a Calcutta children's home), they were in fact created in 1968 by the author Kent Keith as part of a student leadership curriculum. His *10 Paradoxical Commandments* include such masterpieces as:

- The good you do today will be forgotten tomorrow. Do good anyway.
- People are illogical, unreasonable, and self-centered. Love them anyway.
- The biggest men and women with the biggest ideas can be shot down by the smallest men and women with the smallest minds. Think big anyway.

The root of the paradoxical commandments was Keith's effort to embolden weary change agents. The heart of his message was that change is difficult and that change agents can't be engaged for purely selfish reasons. Said Keith:

"I saw a lot of idealistic young people go out into the world to do what they thought was right, and good, and true, only to come back a short time later, discouraged or embittered, because they got negative feedback, or nobody appreciated them, or they failed to get the results they had hoped for. I told them that if they were going to change the world, they had to really love people, and if they did, that love would sustain them. I also told them that they couldn't be in it for fame or glory. I said that if they did what was right and good and true, they would find meaning and satisfaction, and that meaning and satisfaction would be enough. If they had the meaning, they didn't need the glory."

(Keith also had another piece of wisdom: "If you don't care, you're not going to help anyone. Unless you have a deep feeling for the welfare of the people you are supposed to lead, please, stop leading.")

The world needs change agents. Your organization needs change agents. You can be that change agent. Not for the glory or for advancement — you probably won't get either. Not for admiration or even convenience — the path of a change agent can be lonely and often painful as you try to help others see what is possible, prepare for what is inevitable, and let go of what has sustained them thus far. Like great artists, change agents are usually only admired after they are gone. So why bother?

At the heart of his work, Kent Keith was pointing to a bigger motivation, something that today, 40 years later, seems like an old-fashioned notion and certainly not a phrase we use much anymore: brotherly love. As he said, "If you're in it for other people, then helping them will give you satisfaction that having your name in lights could never compete with!"

It is easier to do nothing when you're only concerned about your well-being. Customers in government are often hostages with no choice. Who cares if they are happy? The processes are arduous, cumbersome, and get in the way of helping people. So what? The workplace policies and performance management initiatives are sucking the passion, meaning, and personal satisfaction out of work. What can I do about it? The reality is that these things are all man-made. Humans created them, and humans can change them. Somebody started the ball rolling that got us here. Somebody can start the ball rolling that changes the course.

As the great change agent Margaret Mead said, "Never doubt that a small group of thoughtful, committed citizens can change the world. Indeed, it is the only thing that ever has." Grab the wheel.

With that in mind, I give you the Paradoxical Commandments of Government. These are the reasons why changing your agency is so hard — and why you should do it anyway. Of course, commandments, like hot dogs, only come in packages of 10 (even though buns come in packages of 12), so I had to whittle down the list. I left out some of the pithier ones, such as, "The councilman's cousin is going to get the job; try hard anyway," and "No one will read the report you are working on; write it well anyway." I have also by no means exhausted all the possibilities. In fact, I'd love to hear more commandments from you, my fellow change agents.

The Paradoxical Commandments of Government

1. The reward for doing good work is more work. Do good work anyway.
2. All the money you save being more efficient will get cut from your budget now and forever. Find efficiencies anyway.
3. All the bold reforms you make will be undone by the next administration. Make bold reforms anyway.
4. There is no time to think about improving what we do. Make time anyway.
5. Employees may fight the change every step of the way. Involve them anyway.
6. The future is unpredictable and largely out of your hands. Plan anyway.
7. The press only cares when something goes wrong. Share your success stories anyway.
8. Legal will never let you do it. Simplify it anyway.
9. If you develop your people they will move on to better jobs. Train them anyway.
10. Your ideas will at best make someone else look good and at worst get you ostracized by your co-workers. Share your ideas anyway.

Recommended Reading

Abolishing Performance Appraisals: Why They Backfire and What to Do Instead, by Tom Coens and Mary Jenkins. Berrett-Koehler. 2002.

A Complaint Free World: How to Stop Complaining and Start Enjoying the Life You Always Wanted, by Will Bowen. Harmony. 2007.

Creating a Customer-Centered Culture: Leadership in Quality, Innovation, and Speed, by Robin Lawton. ASQ Quality Press. 1993.

Critical Chain, by Eliyahu M. Goldratt. North River Press. 1997.

Drive: The Surprising Truth About What Motivates Us, by Daniel H. Pink. Riverhead Hardcover. 2009.

Getting Things Done: The Art of Stress-Free Productivity, by David Allen. Penguin. 2002.

The Human Side of Enterprise, by Douglas McGregor. McGraw-Hill Higher Education. 1960.

If We Can Put a Man on the Moon: Getting Big Things Done in Government, by John O'Leary and William Eggers. Harvard Business School Press. 2009

The Leader's Handbook: Making Things Happen, Getting Things Done, by Peter Scholtes. McGraw-Hill. 1997.

Systems Thinking in the Public Sector: The Failure of the Reform Regime ... and a Manifesto for a Better Way, by John Seddon. Triarchy Press. 2008.

ABOUT THE AUTHOR

Ken Miller

Important Stuff:

Ken married way over his head to the incredible Jennifer Miller and has two children. His daughter wants to be a rock star and his son just wants to be better than his dad at everything.

Boring Stuff:

Ken is the founder of the Change and Innovation Agency, a firm dedicated to increasing government's capacity to do more good. Ken has worked with amazing people in the most difficult environments to tackle big issues like:

- How can we best organize the resources of a community to fight poverty?
- How can we overcome the barriers that prevent most inner-city kids from going to college?
- Where's my tax refund?
- How do we make a child abuse hotline as reliable as 911?
- How can we get union workers in psychiatric facilities to say "Thank God it's Monday"?

- How can we transform public assistance offices to serve 40 percent more customers with 20 percent less resources?
- Why is this DMV line so brutally long?

Ken was the deputy director of the Missouri Department of Revenue, where he was part of a transformation effort that reduced the time to issue tax refunds by 80 percent (the fastest in the nation), lowered costs, and cut wait times in motor vehicle offices by half. The agency received a State Quality Award — one of only a handful of government agencies in the country to receive such a distinction. Ken was then named director of performance improvement for Missouri, one of only two states to receive an A grade from *Governing* for Managing for Results.

Ken speaks to thousands of government managers every year spreading his simple but often-ignored message: The only thing standing in the way of the government we want is right between our ears. Our beliefs create our systems. Our systems produce our results. If we want better results in government we need better systems. If we want better systems, we need better beliefs.

Shameless Self-Promoting Stuff:

Ken is the author of two other books, *We Don't Make Widgets: Overcoming the Myths That Keep Government From Radically Improving* and *The Change Agent's Guide to Radical Improvement*, as well as numerous articles and columns on how to improve the performance of government.

Ken was named one of the country's top change agents by *Fast Company* magazine.